# MADE MEN

# MADE MEN

## *Mafia Culture and the Power of Symbols, Rituals, and Myth*

**Antonio Nicaso and Marcel Danesi**

ROWMAN & LITTLEFIELD PUBLISHERS, INC.
Lanham • Boulder • New York • Toronto • Plymouth, UK

Published by Rowman & Littlefield Publishers, Inc.
A wholly owned subsidiary of The Rowman & Littlefield Publishing Group,
Inc.
4501 Forbes Boulevard, Suite 200, Lanham, Maryland 20706
www.rowman.com

10 Thornbury Road, Plymouth PL6 7PP, United Kingdom

British Library Cataloguing in Publication Information Available

**Library of Congress Cataloging-in-Publication Data**
Nicaso, Antonio.
Mafia culture and the power of symbols, rituals, and myth / Antonio Nicaso and Marcel Danesi.
pages cm
Includes bibliographical references and index.
ISBN 978-1-4422-2226-7 (cloth : alk. paper)—ISBN 978-1-4422-2227-4 (electronic)
1. Mafia. 2. Organized crime. I. Danesi, Marcel, 1964- II. Title.
HV6441.N534 2013
364.106—dc23
2013006239

♾™ The paper used in this publication meets the minimum requirements of
American National Standard for Information Sciences Permanence of Paper
for Printed Library Materials, ANSI/NISO Z39.48-1992.

Printed in the United States of America

# CONTENTS

# ACKNOWLEDGMENTS

We would like to express our sincere gratitude for the excellent research conducted for this book by a group of students at the University of Toronto: Mariana Bockarova, Lorraine Bryers, Crow Campbell, Stacy Costa, Sophia Chadwick, and Francesca Marcoccia. Without their painstaking search for relevant information and insightful observations on the facts collected, we would not have been able to bring this book to fruition. Needless to say, any infelicities that this book contains are our sole responsibility. Last but not least, we wish to thank our family members for putting up with us during the writing process. Lucia, Antonella, Massimo, and Emily, this book is dedicated to you.

# INTRODUCTION

The Italian American crime reporter Nicholas Pileggi is widely known for his book *Wise Guys*, which he adapted into the screenplay *Goodfellas* in 1990. *Wise Guys* is about small-time thugs who take part in a robbery for the Mob to gain status within it. Pileggi scripted the fictional events from real-life ones he had come across as a crime reporter. These had evoked rebuke and shock. The book and movie had the opposite effect. They helped spread an image of the modern-day Mafioso as a lethal but nonetheless principled gangster, a "goodfella," who lived by a code of honor, unlike common street thugs.

That glorified image was forged in American popular culture in the 1930s, when many movies showcased the "wise guys" and the exciting and honorable lifestyle they seemed to lead. This image was spread even further after Mario Puzo published his novel *The Godfather* (1969), also based on real-life events. The novel was adapted into a blockbuster movie in 1972, directed by Francis Ford Coppola, becoming one of the most popular and acclaimed films in Hollywood history. *The Godfather* portrays a New York City Mafia family fighting for power over other underworld families. What especially caught America's attention, and stirred its admiration, was the traditional sense of family that the Mafiosi in the movie seemed to possess. America was in the throes of a "postmodern" mind-set in the early 1970s, a worldview that challenged, and continues to challenge, traditional moral and family structures. Although the movie may have had the intent of portraying the heinous nature of Mafiosi, people saw in them something appealing.

No matter how brutal the mobsters were, at the very least, they es-poused the principle of the family as a fundamental social institution. Puzo shared an Academy Award with Coppola for his screenplay. He won another Academy Award with Coppola for the sequel, *The God-father, Part II* (1974). And he cowrote the screenplay with Coppola for the third film in the series, *The Godfather, Part III* (1990).

The myth of mobsters as "goodfellas" and "family and honorable men," created by the movies, has been further entrenched by such television series as *The Sopranos*. But the truth is that the Mob is a ruthless organization. Its concept of the family is a twisted one. But it is difficult to see through the myth when it is being constantly showcased by the mass media. The goal of this book is to deconstruct this myth. We will do so by looking critically and factually at the origin and mean-ing of the code of honor (called omertà in Italian), at its attendant symbols and rituals, and at the lifestyle that it demands. The "wise guy" is, as the mobsters themselves characterize him, a "made man," who is inducted into a criminal family, often by turning his back on his real family, through arcane pseudo-religious rituals, oaths, and symbols that purportedly transform him into a new man.

Although many of the facts, events, and themes in this book can be found scattered throughout the vast literature on organized crime, no coherent treatment exists of how symbolism, ritual, and myth, more than money and power, sustain and fuel Mafia culture. We have written this book because we firmly believe that the best line of attack against the Mafia, and any powerful criminal organization, is to demystify the image of the gangster as a man of honor. Perhaps the best weapon against the Mafia, or at least against the lure that it holds for young people, is to expose its code of honor as something that is largely ficti-tious and self-serving. One of the authors of this book is a Mafia histo-rian and an organized crime expert (Nicaso); the other is an anthropolo-gist and linguist (Danesi).

The term *Mafia* is now used as a general moniker for any under-world criminal organization that displays the same kind of organization-al structure as the original Sicilian Mafia. The latter probably originated from a band of outlaws who saw in violence an opportunity for social advancement, when Sicily was ruled by such outsiders as the Bourbons. The gangsters were feared and, thus, respected by landlords, who took advantage of their presence for their own ends, namely, to maintain control over their own domains. Later on, the outlaws gained unofficial control of part of western Sicily in the 1800s, increasingly extorting the very peasants they claimed to protect. By the end of the century, similar bands of outlaws and misfits started emerging and operating in other parts of southern Italy. This led to the establishment of the Camorra in Naples and the 'Ndrangheta (known at the time as *picciotteria*) in Calabria. In the late 1800s, many gangsters migrated to America. At first, the mobsters simply continued carrying out the same kinds of extortion practices they had left behind in Italy. Prohibition in the 1920s, however, turned the tide for the American Mafia, which took advantage of the situation by turning to bootlegging. At around the same time, Italian dictator Benito Mussolini ruthlessly opposed low-level Mafiosi in Sicily, jailing them and exiling them en masse. Many fled to the United States and eventually became leaders of Cosa Nostra, the name given to the Mafia in America, bolstering its ranks and allowing it to grow considerably in power and reach.

Since the end of World War II, the Mafia in Italy and America has undergone major changes. Its rural base of operation has been moved into urban areas. It has now migrated to online culture. But will it survive? Are more ruthless criminal gangs sprouting up throughout the global village to take its place? We do not entertain these questions directly. Rather, we look at organized criminal culture in general, attempting to explain why it has such a powerful hold on people. Our goal, as mentioned, is to discredit this culture, wherever and however it exists, in the hope that it will deter young people from joining it.

A myriad of books, essays, movies, television documentaries, and Internet sites exist on the Mafia and other criminal organizations. All tell a part of a gruesome and frightening story. Ours is a story as well—a story that seeks to decode the symbols, rituals, and myths that organized criminals use to ensure their continuity. It is a story that has rarely been told in this way, but that we believe is nonetheless important to tell.

# I

# ORIGINS AND ORGANIZATION

Like art and politics, gangsterism is a very important avenue of as-
similation into society.

—E. L. Doctorow (b. 1931)

Released by Hollywood in 1931, *Little Caesar* was a movie adaptation
of the crime novel of the same name, written by American author
William R. Burnett in 1929. It made a star of actor Edward G. Robinson in the role of the vicious gangster Cesare Bandello, nicknamed
"Rico." The way Rico looked, walked, and talked sculpted the mobster
persona into the American popular imagination. Rico became the
prototype of the "wise guy," a ruthless mobster with street savvy and
gritty toughness, but who nonetheless lives by a code of honor. The
movie was fiction, but its characters were fashioned after real-life criminals. They jumped off the screen, shaping people's perceptions of Mafiosi as underdogs and tenacious defenders of ethical principles. Hollywood and the Mafia made perfect partners. They still do. Hollywood
created the *wise guy*, fashioning him after the real-life *furbo* (Italian for
"clever man"). The success of *Little Caesar* made it clear that the movies and criminal culture had formed a dynamic partnership, transforming petty and vicious criminals into larger-than-life figures who lived by
a moral code that many feel has been lost in the modern world.

Because of the numerous gangster movies that followed in the
1930s, a myth surfaced in America, making ersatz heroes out of real
gangsters. "Scarface" Al Capone, Charles "Lucky" Luciano, and others

were brutal thugs, but they became overnight celebrities as interest in the criminals themselves was spread by the movies, perhaps because the movies and the wise guys themselves represented something buried deep in the American psyche. As writer Robert Warshow perceptively writes,

> The experience of the gangster as an experience of art is universal to Americans. There is almost nothing we understand better or react to more readily or with quicker intelligence. In ways that we do not easily or willingly define, the gangster speaks for us, expressing that part of the American psyche [that] rejects the qualities and the demands of modern life, which rejects "Americanism" itself.[1]

Why is the wise guy so alluring? The number of research studies on the social conditions that purportedly lead to gang membership is staggering, as are the theories put forth to explain the allure of criminal lifestyles. Socioeconomic variables, a latent "violence instinct" in modern-day people, and other factors are commonly enlisted by researchers in an attempt to come to grips with the phenomenon of gangs. In our view, these only capture a small part of the truth, since socioeconomic factors, for example, seem to play increasingly diminishing roles today in attracting young people to join gangs. If one looks more closely at the lifestyle of the gangsters, it becomes quite obvious that gangsterism is, as Warshow suggests, a form of art that is performed both in real life and on the silver screen. That is what makes it so appealing and attractive. The art form feeds reality, and, vice versa, reality feeds the art form. From *Little Caesar* to *The Godfather* and *The Sopranos*, gangsterism is portrayed as being more than what it really is—cold-blooded criminality. The Mafiosi know this and have thus adapted accordingly.

Actually, the Mafia has survived through a strategic deployment of art and fiction. It has always portrayed itself as an "honorable society" that lives by a code appropriately called omertà. With this code, murder becomes divine justice; violence, sacred battle; betrayal, sacrilege. Without it, murder would just be gutless homicide; violence, brutal savagery; and betrayal, a banal sellout. Fiction is what allows the Mafia to endure—both the fiction created by the Mafiosi themselves to legitimize their lives and the fiction created by Hollywood and the media. Without these two kinds of fictions, the perception of gangsterism as an art form would dissipate and its lure would be easily excised from the realm of popular culture. Fiction is the main reason why police crusades against the Mafia have proven largely ineffectual in defeating it. Fiction is what allows the gangsters to keep the show going on the stage of life, so to speak.

The first and most basic line of attack against the Mafia is to demystify it, exposing it for what it is—a group of criminals who have fashioned a mystique for themselves based on a code of honor. Once the code is cracked and the mystique is out of the bag, it will evanesce. The history of random street gangs shows that they are generally fleeting, losing their appeal as members age. But organized criminal societies persist because of the strategy of omertà. The code is what binds and keeps members together, attracts new ones, and thus ensures the historical continuity of these societies.[2]


## THE ORIGINS OF THE MAFIA

In Shakespeare's *Romeo and Juliet*, the main protagonists, Romeo Montague and Juliet Capulet, meet and fall madly in love, but they are doomed from the outset, because they belong to warring families. Just the mention of either Montague or Capulet evokes hostile reactions from the opposite side. In the second act, Juliet tells Romeo that a name is a meaningless thing and that she loves the person who bears the name *Montague*, not the Montague name itself and not the Montague family. She asks, "What's in a name? That which we call a rose by any other name would smell as sweet." But Juliet's thought is just the wishful thinking of a young girl in love. A name is everything, since it brings into existence something that would otherwise go unnoticed. The names used by criminal groups are no exception to this rule.

The term *Mafia* refers in its original use to a specific type of secret criminal society in Sicily. Criminal groups stemming from the Mafia operate in other countries, going under various names.[3] The term *Mafia* is now being used as a generic name for criminal organizations, whether Sicilian or not. It has become a metaphor for organized criminal societies. As Mafia historian John Dickie aptly puts it,

> "Mafia" is now one of a long list of words—like "pizza," "spaghetti," "opera," and "disaster"—that Italian has given to many other lan-

guages across the world. It is commonly applied to criminals far beyond Sicily and the United States, which are the places where the Mafia in the strict sense is based. "Mafia" has become an umbrella label for a whole world panoply of gangs.[4]

There was a time when no one ever wanted to pronounce the name of Mafia in Sicily, fearing reprisals and dreading the evil omens that the name was thought to beget. But with the showcasing of Mafiosi on the screen, the term has come to imply something different, even in Italy itself. It has come to symbolize an alternative glorified lifestyle.

Creating an appropriate name is the first step in establishing any criminal group, since it gives the group a sense of identity and distinctiveness. The name *Mafia* is not a word native to the Italian language or the Sicilian dialect. According to a popular legend, the word was coined as an acronym during the Sicilian Vespers, an uprising of Sicilians against the French Capetian House of Anjou headed by the despotic Charles I of Sicily on March 30, 1282. It stood for "*Morte Alla Francia, Italia Anela*" ("Death to France, Italy Cries"). This origin of the term is now largely discredited by historians. The best guess is that the word came into the Sicilian language through an Arabic slang word, *mahyas* ("exaggerated boasting"), *marfud* ("rejected"), or *ma fi* ("It doesn't exist"). The latter word is probably the most likely source of the term *Mafia*, since the Mafia has always denied its existence publicly. In a comprehensive work on the origins of the term, Pasquale Natella claims that the word derives from a Semito-Hamitic source, *maf*, which meant beauty, perfection, and bravery. Natella alleges that the word, modified to *Mafia* in Sicily, may have existed since antiquity and spread throughout the Middle East, reaching Sicily through settlements.[5]

Whatever its origins, the word penetrated the Sicilian language after an 1863 play by Giuseppe Rizzotto and Gaetano Mosca entitled *I mafiusi di la Vicaria* ("The Mafiosi of the Vicaria"). The word *mafiusi* is never mentioned in the actual play, but it was in the title because the audience members understood the allusion implicitly. The word *Mafia* appears a few years later in an 1868 dictionary, where it is revealingly defined as "the actions, deeds, and words of someone who tries to act like a wise guy."[6] As sociologist Diego Gambetta concludes, the term *Mafia* was a largely fictitious word, "loosely inspired by the real thing," that "can be said to have created the phenomenon."[7] It is, in other words, a classic case of what psychologists call confabulation, or the creation of false notions that become believable after the fact, gaining credibility over time. People at the time knew that organized criminal gangs existed, but they were not identified as distinctive. The Sicilian name *mafiusu* was probably being bandied about to provide a name for the gangs, since they espoused a code of secrecy that was consistent with Sicilian culture.[8]

The play is about a fictitious gang of prisoners in Palermo. The gang has a leader; an initiation ritual for new gang members; a code of rules based on silence, called *umirtà* (omertà in modern Italian); and a system for obtaining *pizzu* (a code word for extortion money). In other words, the gang possessed all the hallmark features of the real Mafia. Soon thereafter, the word started appearing throughout Sicily, making its first official appearance in an 1865 report written by Filippo Antonio Gualterio, the prefect of Palermo. As they say, fiction mirrors life, and life mirrors fiction.

Much of modern Mafia slang and the concept of a honor code associated with the Mafia come from the play, as Dickie notes, writing the following:

> The *mafiusi* are a gang of prison inmates whose habits look very familiar in retrospect. They have a boss and an initiation ritual, and there is much talk in the play about "respect" and "humility." The characters use the term *pizzu* for protection payments, as do today's Mafiosi—the word means "beak" in Sicilian. By paying the *pizzu* you are following someone to "wet their beak." If this use of *pizzu* started life as jailhouse slang, it almost certainly entered general use because of the play.[9]

Without names, gangs would be perceived as just a group of hooligans. Through the name, members come to see themselves in more sophisticated ways and thus develop complex symbols and rituals that transform them into miniature cultures, or subcultures, that allow the members to live apart from the mainstream. This is why in police interrogations former gang members actually provide complex, abstract psychological descriptions of themselves as belonging to something meaningful and valuable. Members become interested in understanding their own roles in the gang and why they behave the way they do. Self-esteem increases as gang members move up the gang's hierarchical structure. Like any culture a gang needs a leader; a division of labor and duties; and a set of principles, rituals, and symbols—a code—by which to live.

Criminal groups existed in Sicily long before Rizzotto and Mosca's play provided a collective label for them, but they would have been relegated to the social wayside without a corporate name to remind people of their existence. *Mafia* did the job perfectly. All that was missing was a link to history—a link that would justify the existence of the Mafia as a legitimate cultural reality. This was done by scripting a convenient story connected to Sicilian history, as we shall see later. Storytelling is the essence of confabulation. Confabulated memories seem real and are almost impossible to distinguish from memories of events that actually occurred. Sicily's history of incursions and occupations started with the Greeks, followed by invasions from the Vandals, Byzantines, Arabs, Normans, and Bourbons. This situation is held as being responsible for the creation of secret societies allied to resistance movements. Paul Lunde gives a coherent picture of the conditions that brought about the rise of the Mafia in Sicily as follows:

> From Norman times, the political system in Sicily was feudal. Foreign rulers controlled the island by cultivating the local aristocracy, who obtained concessions in return. The law was whatever the rulers made it. There was no concept of common justice and the peasants were excluded from the political process. They lived desperate lives on the margin of survival. It was from this social milieu that the mafia eventually arose, not as liberators of the oppressed, but as able individuals intent on obtaining their share of wealth and privilege however they could. Traditional Sicilian suspicion of state institutions created the conditions in which the mafia could develop.[10]

The perception of the Mafia as a historically based society has been a disastrous one for Sicily. Already in 1900, Antonino Cutrera, an early anti-Mafia activist and an officer of public security, wrote the following words: "For historical and ethnographic reasons, Sicily has for many years suffered a social vice perpetrated on it by the Mafia. This vice has hindered its social development and has compromised the thrust of its civilization."[11]

Examining Mafia culture without understanding how it is intertwined with Sicilian society and culture would be a futile enterprise.

People from all areas of that society, from the street vendor to police officers, have colluded in one way or another with the Mafia, either for personal gain, to avoid it, to combat it, or to comply with the mobsters because of threats.

Giuseppe Bonanno ("Joe Bananas"), a boss of one of the five infamous families of New York, provides his own theory for the origins of the Mafia. He suggests that the original Mafiosi were Red Shirt volunteers—a theory that he elaborates in his autobiography, writing the following:

> In my grandfather's time, Sicily was under the dominance of the Bourbon dynasty, a royal family of Spanish and French ancestry. Italy itself was like a jigsaw puzzle, with the pieces owned by various powers. Because of the patchwork of foreign domination and internal weaknesses, Italy was the last major country in Europe to be unified under a native ruler. The unification movement was spearheaded by King Victor Emmanuel II and his brilliant prime minister, Cavour. It could not have been accomplished, however, without the leadership and inspiration of the Italian patriot Giuseppe Garibaldi. Garibaldi catalyzed the unification movement by enlisting a volunteer army to liberate Sicily. These volunteers, a motley crew of idealists and zealots, wore a distinctive garb and became known as the Red Shirts. In 1860, Garibaldi's enthusiastic band, some 1,000 strong, landed in Marsala on the west coast of Sicily.[12]

Bonanno's subtext is that among the Red Shirts, there were certain "men of honor" who were able to organize themselves openly, since they were seen as "fighters for the cause." After unification, the Mafiosi became even more unified, laying an even greater stake in Sicilian social and political life. They did this, in part, by portraying themselves as family men, playing on the belief in the pivotal value of bloodlines in Sicilian culture.[13] As Lunde aptly observes, "Nothing is as important to a Sicilian as the ties of blood."[14] Blood lineage assures loyalty and a safety net for the Mafia, which thrives in a culture of vendettas that aim to avenge despoiled honor.

But history paints a different picture. The Mafia gained legitimacy by associating itself, historically, with uprisings against a tyrannical and corrupt state, claiming to be on the side of the peasants. Its crimes against the very peasants it had vowed to protect, however, have be-

come conveniently obfuscated by the Mafiosi throughout time or eliminated from their confabulated narratives. As the acerbic commentator
on human foibles, Mark Twain, so pertinently puts it, "A crime perse-
vered in a thousand centuries ceases to be a crime and becomes a
virtue. This is the law of custom, and custom supersedes all other forms
of law."[15] In a fundamental way, the victims of the Mafia have, through
their own reluctance to speak up against the gangsters, given it strength
and durability. As British author H. G. Wells writes, "Crime and bad
lives are the measure of a State's failure, all crime in the end is the
crime of the community."[16]

Creating a convenient history for itself has been one of the most
effective strategies adopted by the Mafia, since it connects it to Sicily's
past struggles. Fiction is a powerful force in human life. As American
writer Henry Miller so insightfully puts it, fiction "is a part of life, a
manifestation of life, just as much as a tree or a horse or a star. It obeys
its own rhythms, its own laws, whether it be a novel, a play, or a diary.
The deep, hidden rhythm of life is always there—that of the pulse, the
heartbeat."[17]

In the folklore connected to the Calabrian 'Ndrangheta, this heartbeat has been pulsating for a long time, with references to the Garduña
appearing in native Calabrian songs and legends. The Garduña was a
medieval prison gang in Spain that grew into a secret society, carrying
out such crimes as kidnapping, robbery, arson, and murder-for-hire. A
Calabrian legend claims that the Garduña is the precursor of the Sicilian Mafia, the 'Ndrangheta, and the Neapolitan Camorra. It recounts
the story of three Garduña brothers (Osso, Mastrosso, and Carcagnos-
so), who were shipwrecked on the island of Favignana (a Mediterranean island that is part of Sicily). One of the brothers made his way to
Naples to found the Camorra, another to Calabria to set up the 'Ndrangheta, and the third to Sicily to establish the Mafia. Significantly, the
shipwrecked brothers were escapees from the Spanish authorities, having murdered a nobleman who had raped their sister.

But there is no evidence whatsoever to substantiate a link between
the criminal organizations and the three Garduña brothers. The legend
is, itself, a convenient fiction. The view that the 'Ndrangheta is heir to
the Garduña has existed at different times in Calabrian folklore, creating for the criminal group a convenient mystique based on valor and
adventure of the same kind captured by Hollywood pirate movies. Even

the great sixteenth- and early seventeenth-century Spanish novelist Miguel de Cervantes writes about the Garduña in one of his well-known short stories, "Rinconete and Cotadillo."

The Camorra as a structured criminal organization in Naples traces its origins much more prosaically to the eighteenth century, when a gang of mobsters started collecting a tax from prisoners, as well as from prison authorities, to guarantee peace and quiet in the prisons. The term appears in print in an official document of 1735. During the unification of Italy in 1860, the mobsters were hired by Liborio Romano (an important political figure of the times) as vigilantes to keep social order during Garibaldi's mission in Naples. One of its members, Salvatore De Crescenzo, was even made chief of the local faction of the National Guard. As a result, the Camorristi gained amnesty for their previous crimes, boastfully wearing a symbolic pin with the colors of the Italian flag. The operational wing of Camorra, like that of the Mafia, almost became extinct during Italian dictator Benito Mussolini's reign but was revived after World War II, when the Mafiosi allied themselves with other groups in Italian society against communism and communists in the country, allowing it to regain a foothold in Neapolitan and Sicilian politics and society. Today, Camorra and Mafia groups control partitioned territories, forming a kind of parallel government in the two regions (Campania and Sicily).

During the seventeenth century there was, actually, a secret society in Calabria that resembled the contemporary 'Ndrangheta.[18] The word itself has a Greek origin meaning "heroism" and "virtue." The first clear evidence of its existence, however, comes shortly after Italian unification, when the mobsters were hired by powerful stakeholders to threaten their rivals during elections. Unification brought no economic prosperity to southern Italy. Southerners remained impoverished, while squires from northern Italy took possession of large southern estates, imposing heavy taxation throughout the region. The 'Ndrangheta was either formed or heavily reinforced (if it indeed already existed) by groups of Calabrian men who wanted to get rid of the squires, or at least get even by blackmailing or robbing them. The group thus came forward as a kind of Robin Hood gang, preying on the rich, when, in reality, they were aiming to secure financial and political power. It is from that era that a folk culture in Calabria took shape around the 'Ndrangheta, celebrating the 'Ndranghetisti in songs. Gradually, the function and role of the 'Ndrangheta changed, developing into the fearsome brutal society it is today—a fact documented not by folklore, but by crime statistics. The 'Ndrangheta differs from the Sicilian Mafia, the Neapolitan Camorra, and the American Cosa Nostra in that membership is based exclusively on birthright or marriage.

Between the end of the 1970s and the first half of the 1980s, Sicily was the battleground of a Mafia internecine war that upset the equilibrium and relationships within it. The old rules that had moderated disagreements within the ranks and allowed for interclan cohesion were compromised. The many *pentiti* ("informants," literally "those who have repented") who collaborated with the authorities in the 1980s and 1990s opened up the secret society to public scrutiny, substantially dissolving the symbolic power of the Mafia's code of omertà. But the organization survived the attack and still prospers, probably because it continues to adhere to its code as a sacrosanct set of principles that allows its members to feel a strong bond amongst one another.

Omertà is a version of the Italian word *umiltà* ("humility"), which in Sicilian is *umirtà*. It is a code of manly submission to the Mob that requires members to embrace a show of humility and take a vow of silence. Omertà, as Lunde comments, "is a pan-Mediterranean ideal of manhood, going back to the ancient Stoic tradition of ancient Greece and Rome," and is thus bound up "with the larger category of *onore* ("honor")."[19] The code demands a vendetta against anyone who dishonors a Mafioso or his family. The true "made man" must defend the honor of his crime family, which he is expected to protect like his real family. The code of omertà is why the 'Ndangheta and, to some extent the Sicilian Mafia, refer to themselves as the *Onorata Società* (the "Honored Society").

## REINVENTION: COSA NOSTRA

In the late 1800s, gangsters who immigrated to the United States took their Mafia culture with them, but they did not gain much street power until the advent of Prohibition in the 1920s. This allowed them to provide alcohol illegally and thus to profit immensely from bootlegging—the illegal making, selling, and transporting of alcoholic beverages. Also during this time, Mussolini went after Sicilian mobsters with his own form of street justice. Mussolini appointed Cesare Mori, the prefect of Palermo in 1925, to go after the Mafia, giving him special powers to do so. More than 11,000 people were arrested, many of them innocent individuals. They were tried and convicted expeditiously for being either Mafiosi or for having Mafia connections. But Mussolini's "Mafia genocide" strategy did not work as well as expected, since many Mafiosi outwitted the authorities and avoided their roundup net.

As a consequence of Mussolini's dire actions, many gangsters fled to the United States, where they joined other Mafiosi who were already there. Others stayed behind to fight for Sicilian independence, transforming the Mafia once again into a valiant "savior" of the people.[20] Those who emigrated to the United States quickly blended in with the American crime families, which had gained control over so-called speakeasies that had become locales for Mafia bootlegging operations. Speakeasies were the precursors of nightclubs, constituting places for the illegal sale and consumption of alcohol during the Prohibition. The Mafiosi stepped conveniently forward to satisfy a large part of the demand for the alcoholic beverages. Because of the great profit that was involved, different Mafia families battled one another for control of the bootlegging market. Violent gang wars erupted in many large cities, with a resulting carnage. Al Capone of Chicago was probably the era's most famous Mafioso, rising to prominence as a bootlegger. Under his leadership, gang warfare in Chicago reached a frightful peak the morning of February 14, 1929, leading to what has become known, and enshrined by history, as the "St. Valentine's Day Massacre." Seven members of the George "Bugs" Moran gang were viciously assassinated in a North Clark Street garage where bootleg liquor was stored. Police suspected members of the Al Capone gang as the killers but were never able to prove it.

The bootlegging business led to a radical shift in American politics and society. Because the Mafia did not care to whom they sold the liquor, the Prohibition indirectly influenced the evolution of the current egalitarian society, as Lunde observes, stating the following:

> It was during Prohibition that the modern United States, along with American organized crime, was born. Class, racial, and gender barriers began to erode in the fellowship of the speakeasy, where everyone present shared the camaraderie of breaking the law. Politicians, attorneys, and policemen rubbed shoulders with blue collar workers,

gangsters, and entertainers. Al Capone's Cotton Club in Cicero hired black jazz musicians and, by 1927, Chicago had become the jazz capital of the world.[21]

The American Mafiosi also inspired Hollywood. One of the most famous gangster movies of all time, *Little Caesar* (previously mentioned), was likely inspired by Al Capone and his flamboyant lifestyle. Actor Edward G. Robinson attended Capone's trial in 1931 for tax evasion. He wanted to get a close look at Capone for his character model. The 1930s saw a slew of gangster films that permanently entrenched the Mafia into American popular culture. They include *The Public Enemy* (1931), *Scarface* (1932), *G-Men* (1935), *The Petrified Forest* (1936), *Bullets or Ballots* (1936), *Kid Galahad* (1937), *The Last Gangster* (1937), *Racket Busters* (1938), *I Am the Law* (1938), *Angels with Dirty Faces* (1938), and *The Roaring Twenties* (1939). The titles alone provide an annotated anthropology of Mafia culture and its mystique to Americans. The Mafia gangster was replacing the cowboy as the mythic figure of redemption and virtue. After the end of the Prohibition in 1933, the mobsters entered into other illegal paths, including gambling and loan sharking in such major urban areas as New York City and Chicago.[22] The Mafia also played a role in the construction of the early casinos in Las Vegas, again taking advantage of shifts and trends in American culture, thus spreading its tentacles even more deeply into the United States and giving hardworking Italian Americans, who were the real builders of Las Vegas, a bad name by association.[23] Many Italian American pop stars, including Frank Sinatra and Dean Martin, became linked to the Mafia via Las Vegas. Whether this was real or media fiction, it is still part of the popular lore that has always surrounded the American Mafia. As Lunde appropriately points out,

> Probably the place that first comes to mind in association with the topic of casinos and gambling is Las Vegas, which grew with Mafia money during the 1940s. The Hotel Flamingo was opened in Las Vegas in 1947 by Benjamin "Bugsy" Siegel, friend of Meyer Lansky and Charles "Lucky" Luciano. Organized crime made a great deal of money skimming profits from the casinos for 40 years, until the laws regarding gaming were strengthened and it became impossible for anyone with links to organized crime to openly operate in Las Vegas.[24]

The Mafia in the United States had become a self-sustaining criminal organization, with a new identity. It also had a new name—Cosa Nostra. Although the terms *Mafia* and *Cosa Nostra* are often used interchangeably, the two groups are historically distinct. The Sicilian Mafia has roots in the 1800s and Italian unification (as seen earlier). Cosa Nostra, on the other hand, is a crime confederation of American Mafiosi. It is a reinvention. As the most infamous American Mafioso of all time, Al Capone aptly put it when he said, "My rackets are run on strictly American lines and they're going to stay that way."[25] A documented case of this duality is the one associated with Paul Violi, an underboss of the Cotroni crime family in Montreal, during the 1970s. During a conversation with a *picciotto* who had recently emigrated from Sicily, Violi informed him that he could not simply be a member of the clan without showing himself to be worthy of membership for at least a five-year trial period, implying that the Sicilian Mafiosi were perceived as different from the new Mafiosi in North America.

Cosa Nostra, largely created by men of Sicilian birth, still kept ties to the Sicilian Mafia. The term gained popularity through the media after the American *pentito*, Joseph Valachi, referred to the American Mafia as Cosa Nostra while testifying before the Permanent Subcommittee on Investigations of the U.S. Senate Committee on Government Operations in 1963. It was actually the FBI who added the article *La* to the term, referring to it as *La Cosa Nostra*.[26] In Italian, the article is not used. Back in Italy, the authorities did not take the new term seriously at first, mainly seeing it as a label for the American Mob. But, in 1984, it entered the Italian language when the *pentito* Tommaso Buscetta revealed to the anti-Mafia magistrate Giovanni Falcone that it was being used by the Sicilian Mafia as well, which saw an opportunity to reject the traditional term *Mafia* as a mere literary epithet. Buscetta claimed that Cosa Nostra was the real name of the Mafia. Whether or not this was true, it certainly brought the name to center stage in the world of organized crime.

Cosa Nostra, unlike the Sicilian Mafia and certainly the 'Ndrangheta, is an equal opportunity employer. In the latter, mainly men descended from 'Ndrangheta families can be admitted as members. This rule has actually been a double-edged sword for the gang. It is counterproductive because it fosters internecine warfare. On the other hand, it minimizes the risk of infiltration by unwanted individuals and defection by members. "Blood is thicker than water" is a fundamental principle of the 'Ndrangheta. Cosa Nostra has no such requirement.


## THE DISPLAY OF POWER

The sense of belonging and self-worth that comes with joining a criminal gang exceeds the desire for wealth. Mafia fugitives could enjoy a life of luxury. Instead, they remain in their gang, hunted down and in danger of being arrested or killed by dissidents and other gangs, to maintain their criminal status. "Being someone" is a more compelling incentive than any amount of money. The Mafia is a power trip, as the character Rico Bandello in *Little Caesar* emphasizes repeatedly in the movie.

Intimidation (real and perceived) is a way of gaining power over people. It is directed at extortion victims, *pentiti*, relatives of *pentiti*, judges, police officials, and at anyone who gets in their way. It is as important as is the actual use of violence. Marks left on dead bodies indicating the nature of the victim's injustice toward the Mafia, artifacts (letters, symbols) left near the cadaver, menacing *sguardi* ("looks"), *gesti* ("gestures"), and other signature strategies are all intimidation tactics.[27]

Alliances with other criminal groups are also part of ensuring power, even though such alliances go contrary to the origins of criminal societies. The traditional source of revenue for the Mafia has been extortion. Today, it is narcotics trafficking that provides it with its greatest source of income. This new line of business requires cooperation. The Mafia has, in fact, established a transportation network with other gangs for the trafficking of heroin and cocaine. The extent of the close relationship between the Mafia and Colombia's Medellin drug cartel, for instance, first became apparent with the November 2, 1989, indictment of twelve people in Miami linked to the Mafia. The defendants were accused of shipping cocaine by train and car from Miami to Philadelphia and New York. Among those indicted were a member of the Sicilian Mafia and a Barranquilla drug group member, a group directly linked to the cartel. In 2008, a joint Italian, Mexican, and American investigation uncovered a link between the Calabrian 'Ndrangheta and the Mexican Gulf Cartel, leading to the arrest of 507 individuals and the seizure of more than $60 million in U.S. currency and of large amounts of cocaine, heroin, and other narcotics.[28]

The display of power with strategies like these allows the Mafia to recruit individuals, known as "middlemen," who fear violent repercussions from the Mob if they do not follow orders. In the 1989 case, once the drugs were in the United States, an intricate network of pizzerias and pizza joints was used to distribute them. The eateries served as fronts for the Mob, providing them with legitimate sources of income, as well as a locus for gaining a foothold in the community. But their real function was to provide a system for recruiting middlemen to push and sell the drugs in small quantities. The middlemen were typically illegal aliens from Italy or Italian Americans who were attracted to the Mob lifestyle as "wannabes." As legal scholar Jonathan Kwitny observes, the strength of middlemen and intergang partnerships can be discerned in the stated philosophy of the Mafia as *"una mano lava l'altra"* (literally "one hand washes the other," meaning "I'll do this for you, if you do that for me").[29] This tit-for-tat strategy is also the reason why bribery of officials and the corruption of politicians are typical Mafia tactics.[30] As the fictitious Don Corleone of *Godfather* fame put it, mirroring the true mind-set of the Mafia, "A lawyer with his briefcase can steal more than a hundred men with guns."

An inside look at the power strategies of the Mafia comes from a series of indictments stemming from a federal crackdown on organized crime called "Iron Tower." The investigation started as two separate probes. They were subsequently merged into one when it became apparent that there was an international component to the operations involving a Sicilian connection. The investigation focused on several New Jersey members of the Mafia. In 1988, the probe resulted in the arrest of more than 200 suspected Mafiosi and middlemen in the United States, Italy, Spain, and the Dominican Republic. The impact of Iron Tower—an appropriate metaphor for how the Mafia conducted its operations in an "iron-fisted" way within its "tower" of operations—virtually destroyed the illegal operations.

Although several members of the cartel lived and conducted their activities in the New Jersey and Philadelphia areas, the headquarters was Café Giardino, a restaurant in Brooklyn. Recording devices and telephone wiretaps were used to record the conversations, most of which were in the Sicilian dialect. The use of dialect is part of the power trip, as we will soon discuss. The dialect is a perfect language for maintaining secrecy, spoken only by those in the know. It is, like other symbol systems used by the Mafia, *una cosa nostra.*

While Iron Tower was a major victory for law enforcement, the Mafia was no stranger to attacks from the law. It has always rebounded quickly. Leadership roles left vacant because of the prosecutions were, in fact, filled promptly by others in the gang. In the end, Iron Tower did not demolish the Mafia fortress; it only made a few dints in it. The Mafia is not just about drugs and wealth; it is about symbolic power that keeps members bound together at all times—good and bad. As Lunde has indicated, criminal societies have staying power because they have group-preserving structure and are able to create a mystique about themselves—a mystique that has bonding strength:

> Organized crime, however defined, shares a few basic characteristics, whatever the differences among individual groups and the cultures that produced them. They have in common durability over time, diversified interests, hierarchical structure, capital accumulation, reinvestment, access to political protection, and the use of violence to protect their interests. Successful organized crime groups each have their own mystique, ensuring solidarity and loyalty through shared ethnicity, kinship, or allegiance to a code of behavior. [31]

We would add one other attribute to Lunde's list as a factor giving the Mafia its longevity and perseverance—a sense of historical succession. The Mafia's domination of Sicily is traced by some back to the so-called *gabellotti* ("bailiffs") of the feudal period. These were men trusted by the aristocracy to collect taxes from the rural peasantry and manage their estates. They were important figures because the landowners were rarely around, living in cities. When the social system changed, the *gabellotti* remained, forming a proto-criminal gang that continued to collect "taxes," for their own pockets. After Italian Unification in 1861, they emerged as leaders of crime families, which were evolving into a form of shadow government, able to influence social, economic, and political life in Sicily. They controlled to whom the farmers sold their produce and the markets that acquired it. They controlled the materials that came into the island. Through intimidation and bribery, they were able to influence whoever was given a government job and infiltrate various legal and judicial institutions.

Revolt by people against the crime gangs is also rarely effective for the same reasons that legal actions against them are usually futile. The first major American Mafia incident occurred in New Orleans in 1890. A Sicilian crime family was being constantly harassed by the local chief of police, David Hennessy. As a result, he was murdered. When the mobsters were tried, they bribed witnesses. To everyone's shock, they were acquitted. Anti-Italian fervor erupted, and a lynch mob went to the jailhouse. The mob shot or hanged the released men. The incident was thought at the time to have annihilated the Mafia in the United States, but it did not. The only thing that the incident achieved was to introduce the term *Mafia* in the United States, as newspapers discussed it at length. The newspapers also were drawn to intergang warfare. An epidemic of Mafia violence surfaced in the early 1930s. Mafia bosses and their soldiers were slaughtered on a daily basis, with few ruling their families for more than a couple months at a time. The Lucchese family, alone, went through four bosses in 1930. The media loved it, since it sold newspapers and tabloids.

In the middle of this bloodbath, "Lucky" Luciano saw the advantages that alliances brought. He simply realized that there was strength in numbers, not in the hegemony of one crime family over others, gained through warfare. His new model for Cosa Nostra was a multi-family syndicate that would approve activities nationwide. Luciano's accomplishments are now the stuff of legend. His *furbizia* ("cleverness" or "wise-guy-ness") was unparalleled before or since. He was even crucial in getting a deal struck between the U.S. military and the Sicilian Mafia that would help the Allies in their invasion of Sicily in 1943.[32] The Allies, aided by the mobsters, were welcomed as liberators. The imprisoned Mafiosi under Mussolini were released from jail or returned from exile. By the end of World War II, the Mafia had become a major crime syndicate operating in both Sicily and the United States.

In Italy, the Mafia formed secret alliances with leading political figures in the Christian Democratic Party, the dominant political force in Italy for four decades following the war. With support at the highest echelons of the political hierarchy, the Mafia was able to expand its influence over the entire country, not just Sicily. It was not until it overreached its boundaries that the judicial system found the nerve and courage to unravel the Mafia's massive influence over the entire Peninsula. The Mafia had declared an open war on the Italian state through a series of car bombings of Italian political figures. The outrage from the public forced the government to lend concrete support to honest, crusading anti-Mafia judges and officials. But, as it turned out, it was impossible to stamp out the Mafia.

The Mafia, 'Ndrangheta, Cosa Nostra, the Camorra, and other major criminal gangs perceive themselves as genuine societies, possessing a pseudo-value system that prizes honor, respect, and family ties—all of which are seen as lacking in the contemporary secular world, in which the philosophy of "anything goes" is seen to prevail. They are glorified for this by movies and television programs. This is a convenient myth for the Mafia, obfuscating what it really is—a cancer spreading throughout the global village. The Mafia has been very bad for Italians. In New Orleans, where the first Sicilian immigrants made their home, the mayor openly called them the most idle, vicious, and worthless people he had ever encountered. He publicly stated that he wanted to wipe out every one of them from the face of the earth. As social scientist Dwight Smith suggests, the Italians became part of a convenient alien conspiracy backlash that was really xenophobia disguised as outrage against criminality.[33] This only exacerbated the situation. The Italian communities accepted protection from the criminals because of the public outcry against them, even though most of them worked diligently and contributed significantly to American society. The American Mafiosi soon found new ways to protect their own countrymen from corrupt police forces and others who wished to exploit them. In reality, however, the primary target of the gangsters was the countrymen.

Already at the turn of the twentieth century, *La Mano Nera* ("The Black Hand") had emerged as an extortion racket. Victims would receive a letter telling them to give the sender a certain sum of money or else risk death from a secret "Black Hand Society." The letters were always signed with a black handprint. The Black Hand terrorized the immigrants. One of the most infamous Black Handers was Ignazio Saietta, also known as "Lupo the Wolf." Saietta came from Italy to live with his brother-in-law, Nicholas Morello, who had built his own criminal operations into a thriving New York Mafia crime family that was eventually able to challenge all other gangs for territorial control. Saietta joined forces with Morello to carry out Black Hand operations. The growth of Morello's power illustrates why the American Mafia became (and still is) so successful. He started out seemingly protecting his own community before exploiting it and turning the innate distrust of authority among the immigrants into a self-serving barrier of silence. He used Black Hand tactics to expand into other criminal areas, giving Morello an edge over his rivals. Black Hand terror was real. In 1908, there were more than 400 documented cases of Black Hand extortion in New York. Between 1910 and 1914, there were more than 100 murders attributed to the Black Hand.

The power of the symbolism did not go unnoticed by the early moviemakers. Indeed, an early film short, *The Black Hand* (1906), originally in Italian (*La Mano Nera*), became highly popular. Another movie of the same name, *La Mano Nera*, came out in 1909. It was a stark portrait of the deleterious effects Mafia culture had brought to the United States, based on the funeral of Italian American police detective Giuseppe (Joe) Petrosino, who was the first police officer to understand the need for American police forces to cooperate with Italian ones in weeding out the Mafia. Petrosino became an effective crusader against Black Hand operations in New York. As an Italian-speaking officer born in Italy, he understood the nuances of the Italian language and the code of honor used by the criminals. No one was convicted of the murder of Petrosino—a killing that was carried out while Petrosino was secretly visiting Palermo to orchestrate a cooperative anti-Mafia crusade. His body was returned to New York and his funeral attended by more than 250,000 people. The movie is not a gangster movie. Along with the other ones, it constitutes a filmic snapshot of the growing brutality of *la malavita* ("the bad life") that Mafia culture entailed. It warned of things to come at the same time that it captured a growing gangster ethos that both repelled and appealed to movie audiences.

Cosa Nostra has become a major player in shaping American history.[34] The JFK murder, for instance, is entangled with a Mafia subtext—a fact noted and popularized by American director Oliver Stone in his blockbuster 1991 movie *JFK*, a controversial interpretation of the events surrounding the assassination of President John F. Kennedy, involving collusion among the Mafia, FBI, and CIA. Stone followed this up with *Natural Born Killers* (1994), a satire about America's fascination with crime and violence. Through dummy firms and businesses, Cosa Nostra now controls numerous entertainment places, construction companies, food distribution and food services, large chunks of the garbage business, and much more. It has corporate structure. It feeds on fear and corruption, sustaining itself through its display of power.[35] Cosa Nostra is also highly adaptive to change, expanding its activities into the new industrial and technological areas of the contemporary world, as well as engaging in financial market manipulation. Cosa Nostra continues to be an organized criminal threat to American society.

Strengthening Cosa Nostra is the fact that it opened its doors to non-Sicilian gangsters. By an agreement with the largest family in New York City, the Sicilian Mafia was granted permission to take over parts of the lucrative heroin trade. Since then, the syndicate, just like a legitimate corporation, has grown, cooperating with other organized crime groups throughout the world in the trafficking of drugs. As already mentioned, its power was first brought into public light during the so-called Pizza Connection case in the early 1980s.[36] The case led to the FBI working closely with the Italian police, the Royal Canadian Mounted Police, and Colombian authorities. Since then, FBI investigations have resulted in successful prosecutions of most of the families and the reduction of syndicate wealth through the aggressive use of asset forfeiture, undermining the Mafia's financial power base. The FBI also developed an effective investigative technique called *enterprise theory*, which stipulates that "association in fact" can be used in a prosecution or a civil proceeding. Evidence of criminal acts is gathered to establish the criminality of an enterprise and also of individuals associated with it. But despite such legal measures and tools, the tentacles of Cosa Nostra have penetrated way too deeply into every aspect of social, economic, and cultural life. When Bernardo Provenzano, the alleged *capo dei capi* ("boss of bosses") of Cosa Nostra, was captured on April 11, 2006, in Corleone, Italy, after many decades on the run, anti-Mafia prosecutor Pietro Grasso put it as follows:

> He was protected by professionals, politicians, businessmen, law enforcers. We found all of them in our investigations. Provenzano was under the protective umbrella of his criminal colleagues and, more importantly, by entire sectors of society. It was not a single politician who served as his protector all those years. It was the political system.[37]

It will take a different kind of approach to eradicate the Mafia. It is relevant to note that in 2010, the FBI uncovered an alleged scheme involving the removal of debris at Ground Zero in New York that was directed by several members of the Colombo crime family of New York. An indictment alleged that a Mob-controlled trucking company paid kickbacks to secure a subcontract with a demolition company working at Ground Zero.[38]

The Mafia's infiltration into the world of politics has been well documented. But its goal is not to replace the state. Rather, it seeks to manipulate the political system for its own profit. Sicilian politicians cultivated criminals early on in Mafia history to deliver the vote at election time; the Mafia was thus able to gain access to the island's political system. For many years after World War II, its most significant relationship was with the Christian Democrat Party, a fact brought out by the movie *Il Divo* (2008), which deals with longtime Christian Democrat leader Giulio Andreotti's links with the Mafia. With the party's demise as a political force in Italy, the bosses turned to a new party, *Forza Italia*, a party that also walked a fine line in its relationship with shady characters. One of the founders of *Forza Italia* was convicted for collusion with the Mafia.

## ORGANIZATION

Like the military or large corporations, the Mafia has been able to endure in large part because it has adopted a model of hierarchical organization. This includes a *capofamiglia*, or just capo ("boss of a family"); a *sottocapo* ("underboss"); a *consigliere* ("counselor"); a *capodecina* (one of a number of lieutenants responsible for ten or more men); and foot soldiers called *picciotti* ("little ones"), who are low-ranking enforcers. The capo's presence and word, like that of a CEO, are enough to bring about a business arrangement on terms favorable to him. In the 1990s, a huge shopping center was planned in a town called Villabate. The local Mafia became involved in the project with a developer from northern Italy, acquiring the land and removing bureaucratic obstacles by pulling all the right strings. The capo overlooked the whole project, just like a normal CEO would. He controlled 20 percent of the hired employees and 30 percent of the office space. But unlike real CEOs, the boss was a gangster, receiving large kickbacks for eliminating the convoluted red tape that surrounds such projects in Italy. Things seemed to go according to plan, until the authorities stepped in, arresting the principal players in the corrupt scheme. The shopping center was never finished. The case showed conspicuously how paralyzing to social growth and development the Mafia's continued presence and power is.

The capo rules as the family head and makes all final decisions. In holding the top position, the boss gets a "cut" of all family income garnered by the lower-ranking members. The *sottocapo* is appointed by the boss. He is the second in command. His main duty is to pass along information, when necessary, and manage the everyday affairs of the family. The *sottocapo* will take over as "acting boss" if the capo is jailed or murdered. He is also a major voice in decision-making. The consigliere is the next one down the ladder. He is a mediator of disputes or of business between his family and other Mafia families. He also carries out bribery activities, for example, political payoffs. He is a trusted family member who holds a fair degree of power but is not involved in the conduct of street-level operations. At the bottom are the soldiers, or *picciotti*, who carry out the threats, brutality, and violence that get the job done. To become a soldier in the traditional Mafia, the member is expected to be of Sicilian background. As we have already seen, the American Cosa Nostra changed all this. But in all criminal organizations, the new member is accepted in the family only via an initiation ceremony, which includes a binding oath of loyalty that, if broken, will be punished by death.

Like any corporation, every Mafia family has "associates" with whom business is carried out, even though they are not members of the specific clan. Associates are lawyers or public officials who are hired as go-betweens between the family and mainstream society, allowing the crime family to gain access to legitimate sectors of society. But the basis of operations of the Mafia has not changed throughout the years. It was always protection through extortion, which, as Lunde astutely observes, has provided the "plots for many gangster movies."[39] Mafiosi are generally prohibited by their own code of honor to commit vulgar theft and robberies. They abhor those who do. The *pizzo* is perceived by them to be much like a legal tax system, not a form of extortion. They see the state as a criminal organization, competing with it for a stake in the control of the money flow and reflecting the popular view expressed by the great theologian St. Augustine of Hippo it in the fourth century, "For what are states but large bandit bands, and what are bandit bands but small states?"[40] Taxation ensures that people are protected; by extension, so does the *pizzo*. Indeed, if a target is robbed by thugs, the Mafiosi will actually go after them and make them pay for their vulgarity. As the first *capo di tutti i capi* ("the boss of all bosses"), Vito Cascio Ferro (1862–1943), known as Don Vito, put it, "Don't ruin people with absurd demands for money. Offer your protection instead. Help them prosper in business and they'll not only be happy to pay the *pizzu*, but they'll kiss your hand in gratitude."[41]

Not all criminal organizations have the same type of hierarchical structure. In the 'Ndrangheta, the basic family clan is called the *'ndrina*, which is made up of blood relatives. Several 'ndrine form a *locale* (a large clan), which has jurisdiction over an entire town or area within a large urban center. The head of the family is called *capobastone* (literally "the head pole or staff"), who has command over the entire clan. Like corporate managers, *capobastoni* meet once a year in a sanctuary dedicated to the Madonna outside the village of San Luca, a small town near Locri. As John Lawrence Reynolds aptly points out, unlike the pyramid structure of the Mafia, the 'Ndrangheta has its basis completely in bloodlines:

> The combination of tight structure and family blood provides the 'Ndrangheta with an enormous ability to maintain both secrecy and loyalty, consolidated through carefully arranged marriages between 'ndrinas. Nothing in Sicilian or Calabrian culture is more sacrosanct than family, and where linkages exist through marriage it would be an act of serious dishonor for one family to perform any act that would threaten the security of a related family.[42]

Major non-Italian criminal syndicates also thrive because of structure, including the Russian Mafia (or Mafiya), the Japanese Yakuza, the Chinese Triads, and many others. This includes not only the assignment of specific roles to members, but also the adoption of customs and symbols that allow members to determine loyalty and adherence to the group in terms of a code. These are the basic elements that constitute a criminal culture. We discuss these throughout this book.

Differences among the organizations are felt as necessary to keep their identities distinct. The Camorra and the Mafia, for instance, operate differently for this reason. The Camorra either shuns or discourages the same sense of kinship bonds. Family ties are important, but they are not essential. Virtually anyone can join the Camorra and rise to the top. All he has to do is prove his mettle through brutal street violence. This makes the Camorra an ideal recruitment group for dispossessed youth aiming to make a lot of money quickly or put forth a kind of "intimidating persona" on the streets of Naples. The Camorra also does not require an initiation ceremony, as do the Mafia, the 'Ndrangheta, and other criminal organizations.[43] Nevertheless, the organization does require killing someone to prove one's mettle and allegiance, which is, clearly, an initiation ritual.

In recent times, the Mafia and other criminal organizations have had to adapt to changes in society, like every other type of business. Increasing pressure and prosecution by the FBI, and in Italy by crusading anti-Mafia magistrates, have led to a rash of convictions. This has brought about the creation of new positions in the organizational structure, including the "family messenger" and the "street boss." The former passes on orders from the leadership to middle management in a low-key way, to avoid detection; the latter temporarily takes over the family if the boss is unavailable to the family and a new boss has not been appointed. The Mafia survives, not only because it stakes a claim to historical validity, but also because it knows how to adapt to change.[44] It continues to have large appeal as a kind of folk devil who is nonconformist, "repudiating the virtues of the world," as French playwright Jean Genet eloquently describes the power of the outlaw in modern societies, a heroic folk figure who "agrees to organize a forbidden universe."[45] Mafia culture epitomizes this "forbidden universe," which philosopher Michel Foucault calls a universe based on a "lyricism of marginality" and inhabited by "the great social nomad, who prowls on the confines of a docile, frightened order."[46]

# 2

# HONOR

Since an intelligence common to us all makes things known to us and formulates them in our minds, honorable actions are ascribed by us to virtue, and dishonorable actions to vice; and only a madman would conclude that these judgments are matters of opinion, and not fixed by nature.

—Cicero (106–43 BCE)

They say that there is no honor among thieves, but it is precisely a self-serving notion of honor on which Mafia culture is based. As the Mafia historian John Dickie observes, a large part of the ability of the Mafia to endure is the myth of its origins in a chivalric code—a code of omertà based on a concept of honor and retribution for injustices.[1] This is the subject of Pietro Mascagni's marvelous 1890 opera *Cavalleria rusticana* ("Rustic Chivalry"), which deals with the rustic ethos of Sicilian culture. Based on a play by the Italian Romantic writer Giovanni Verga, it focuses on the violent behavior that arises when people are under great emotional strain seeking to make sense of their lives. In such situations, for guidance, people rely on a set of principles that espouse honor, respect, and fidelity. Mascagni was not Sicilian. He was Tuscan. As an outsider, he was likely captivated by the emotional power of the Sicilian code of honor that he saw imprinted in the facial expressions of common people and deeply entrenched in their daily culture.

It is no coincidence that the opera's famous intermezzo was used by director Martin Scorsese in the slow-motion title of *Raging Bull* (1980), a movie about pride and honor, Italian style. Coppola also used various excerpts from the opera for his *The Godfather, Part III*. In the film's climax, a Mafioso is seen stalking his victim in the Teatro Massimo in Palermo, where Mascagni's opera is being performed on stage. Again, it seems that life and art mirror one another, influencing one another constantly.

Bonds of family and friendship are strong in Sicily, especially given the hundreds of years of invasion and foreign rule that have constantly undermined the Sicilians' trust in officials and authorities. Family can be trusted; others cannot. That deeply rooted belief is what makes the Mafia code of omertà so emotionally powerful, for both the Mafiosi and their victims. The code puts forth its own system of justice, warning members not to dishonor themselves by cooperating with the government and outsiders. Any injustice against a clan member is to be taken care of within and by the clan. Sicily's tradition of private justice is what gives omertà a powerful psychological grounding. As the French social philosopher Alexis de Tocqueville aptly observes, "It is the dissimilarities and inequalities among men [that] give rise to the notion of honor; as such differences become less, it grows feeble; and when they disappear, it will vanish too."[2] The code of honor implicit in the *Cavalleria rusticana*, not to mention many Hollywood gangster films, is now part of an unconscious mythic tale spun about the Mafia. The Mafia defines itself in terms of this code of rustic chivalry, tapping into the very ethos of Sicilians. "Today," writes Dickie, "it is impossible to tell the story of the mafia without reckoning with the power of that same myth."[3]

## OMERTÀ

From the dawn of time, humans have organized their social relations and affairs into codes of conduct to impart continuity and fluidity to these relations. Culture is a network of codes that regulate human beings and provide guidelines on conduct and interactions. Some codes stipulate the fundamental values shared by members of the culture and by which they should live. All organizations also develop codes for themselves, explicit or implicit. Codeless organizations are an oxymoron. The Mafia continues to exist as an institution because of its code of omertà; without such a code, it would collapse. Criminal codes are typically kept secret. What is kept secret is meaningful; if revealed, it is believed to imperil the group, and the revealer is punished severely. As British writer Aldous Huxley writes, secrecy is a powerful motivating force in human groupings: "To associate with other like-minded people in small, purposeful groups is for the great majority of men and women a source of profound psychological satisfaction. Exclusiveness will add to the pleasure of being several, but at one; and secrecy will intensify it almost to ecstasy."[4] In a conversation with another mobster in 1998, Carmine Alvaro, a 'Ndrangheta boss, was recorded saying the following: "Let me say one thing. The 'Ndrangheta is ugly for those outside of it. . . . But the 'Ndrangheta is extremely beautiful because it has the most beautiful rules. If anything goes, everything comes apart. Chaos results. Things must be done according to the rules" (translation ours).[5]

The Mafia code is especially powerful and compelling because it taps into the *cavalleria rusticana* psychology of the Sicilian people, which also espouses an implicit principle of vendetta—anyone whom the Mob has targeted or persecuted and who seeks recourse to legal authority against the Mob is branded as a coward, meriting reprisal. This principle reflects a common attitude in various Latin and Mediterranean societies, that recourse to the law for offenses involving personal insult is unmanly. In fact, the Sicilian word for omertà (*umirtà*) connotes not only humility, but also manliness. "The marks of the true Mafioso," writes Lunde, "are that he speaks little, makes each word count, and maintains a grave and dignified presence at all times, even under extreme provocation."[6] This ideal of manliness goes back to ancient times when the Stoics extolled it, believing that a "real man" should be free from senseless passion and should calmly accept all occurrences as the unavoidable result of fate. A real man, according to omertà, will defend his honor and that of his family, no matter what personal consequences this will incur. In real chivalric times, the appropriate action for restoring lost honor was the duel or some other form of vengeful retribution involving physical conflict. Today, it is death by assassination. The code thus has a practical value for the Mafiosi—it hampers police investigations, because informants have been either sworn to silence by the code or else fear reprisal from the Mob. Ordinary citizens similarly fear retaliation, knowing full well that they or their loved ones would be punished severely if they broke the silence.

A perfect example of this mind-set is found in a conversation between a Mafioso and his young son that was intercepted by police surveillance in 2001 in a town near Rome. The relevant part of the conversation is cited in what follows:

> *Father*: Did you understand what Mafioso means?
> *Son*: Uh?
> *Father*: What it means?
> *Son*: It's when . . .
> *Father*: Ok, you have to listen very, very, very carefully to what I am going to tell you. There exists a concept of the law . . . the law exists . . . there are policemen, judges . . . there exists a concept of the family . . . do you follow, do you understand? Well, a [real] family never turns to the law, but seeks justice on its own terms. Do you understand what I'm saying? If someone does something against you, I would never go to the police and blab to them. "Someone has done something to my son." I will get the person responsible and kill him! Do you understand how it works? That's what the Mafia is all about.[7] (translation ours)

The honor code of the Mob exacts total and complete obedience and compliance from members. Dickie puts it as follows:

> Honor accumulates through obedience: In return for what they call "availability," individual Mafiosi can increase their stock of honor and, in doing so, gain access to more money, information, and power. Belonging to Cosa Nostra offers the same advantages as does belonging to other organizations, including the achievement of aspirations, an exhilarating sense of status and comradeship, and the chance to pass responsibility, moral or otherwise, upward in the direction of their bosses. All of these are ingredients of mafia honor.[8]

Codes require symbols. Without symbols, a code will have virtually no meaning, as de Tocqueville points out. The Mafia code is replete with symbolism, transforming a mere criminal gang into a self-contained culture, imparting to its members a sense of belonging to something meaningful, and thus producing internal cohesion and a sense of identity that allows mobsters to set themselves markedly apart from the riffraff, which includes not only random gangs and street thugs, but also virtually everyone else.

As in any cult or secret society, one has to earn admittance into the group by endorsing and assimilating the code and then proving his mettle and commitment through some initiation rite. Outsiders are considered irrelevant, at best, and cowards or disposable bodies, at worst. Traitors to the code are, needless to say, the most despised, because they have broken the oath of silence, honor, and respect. The code is a formidable emotional tool for engendering and guaranteeing allegiance to the Mafia. Belonging is perceived to be a privilege that only real men can earn. The Mafia code is not, of course, a legal document; it is a "legitimizing" document, complete with its own attendant norms, principles of justice, and set of lifestyle rules that are reminiscent of the honor codes of the past, especially those of medieval chivalric groups and secret societies like the Freemasons.[9]

Membership in a Mafia clan produces a shared illusion of invulnerability and personal empowerment, and this illusion provides members with the impetus to take extraordinary risks and rationalize warnings and potential danger signs. In other words, membership produces an "empathy of belonging" based on the belief that agreement on issues is unanimous among all members. This puts the individual member in a position to ignore the broader ethical implications of what he does. Once a wise guy, always a wise guy. Like the three musketeers of fictional narrative lore, wise guys live by the creed of "one for all, all for one." This puts pressure on members who stray from the clan's belief system, who will inevitably be marginalized, ostracized, and even eliminated. Members feel compelled to shelter and protect the clan, and especially the leader, from adversities of all kinds. In other words, the code taps into a latent "village psychology," described so eloquently by French writer Jean de La Bruyère in 1608:

> The town is divided into various groups, which form so many little states, each with its own laws and customs, its jargon and its jokes. While the association holds and the fashion lasts, they admit nothing well said or well done except by one of themselves, and they are incapable of appreciating anything from another source, to the point of despising those who are not initiated into their mysteries.[10]

Initiation rites into "the mysteries," as de la Bruyère calls them, are compulsory and perceived as being of the utmost importance. A new member shows allegiance to the clan and its leader by undertaking specified actions (including murder), donning appropriate symbols (for example, marks on the body), and performing particular rituals. He must also take a specific oath of loyalty and assume the duty of patrolling a territory determined to be his turf. Finally, he must learn to use various signs, signals, and words so as to be able to communicate meaningfully with others and, at times, furtively with the other members in the presence of outsiders.

The enormous emotional power of the code and its attendant symbols and practices, with their underlying chivalric connotations, has more to do with Mafia longevity than any of the traditionally accepted socioeconomic and sociopolitical causes.[11] A recurrent reason why young people join gangs was encapsulated in the response given by one of them to a researcher for this book investigating the phenomenon of gang membership in general: "It's cool, man! Nobody, messes around with us!"[12] Glorified by movies and other media, gang membership affords many young people the opportunity to look and act tough, just for the sake of it, or, more accurately, for the look of it. One thinks, for instance, of the media fixation with ghetto teen gangs in the 1950s—a phenomenon captured brilliantly by the 1957 musical *West Side Story*.[13] And, of course, movies like *The Godfather* and television series like *The Sopranos* add to the mystique of manly honor that is intrinsic to the constitution of all criminal organizations.

The authorities are, of course, well aware of the power of omertà. In its 2003 annual report, the Commissione Parlamentare Antimafia characterized the 'Ndrangheta as a society held together by internal rules, hierarchies, and statutes that assign "dignity" to its actions, assuring the unabashed faithfulness of the initiate. Connecting to instinctive human values is, arguably, what makes the code compelling. The symbol used by the 'Ndrangheta to represent itself is, in fact, an ancient one connected to human origins—the "tree of knowledge"—that is divided into its various parts: the tree base, representing the head of the clan or *capobastone*, who exerts power of life and death over members; the trunk (*fusto*), representing the *sgarristi*, who are the spinal column of the clan; the branches (*rami*), or *camorristi*, who are responsible for organizing activities; the smaller branches (*ramoscelli*), who are the foot soldiers, known as the *picciotti*; and the leaves (*foglie*), which stand for recruits. The leaves that fall to the ground are the betrayers who, because of their disloyalty, are destined to die.[14] The 'Ndrangheta continues to thrive, as those familiar with its operations assert, because of the emotional influence of its code.[15] The symbol of the tree of knowledge as used by the 'Ndrangheta was first made public by testimony given in a Calabrian court in 1897, by a certain Pasquale Trimboli, and then published in *Cronaca di Calabria*, a weekly newspaper, on March 11, 1897.

Throughout the world, the family is the traditional institution where values are learned and perpetuated.[16] Mafia culture is a culture stylized to resemble the extended family structure, but the concept of family espoused by the Mafia is an artificial and self-serving one. The movie *Il capo dei capi* (2007), which tells the story of infamous Mafioso Totò Riina, reveals the distorted view of family that the Mafia upholds on the surface. Riina has no respect for the lives of others, apart from those in his immediate circle of friends, family, and acquaintances. He endorses family and Catholic values openly but ends up perverting both. In the movie, Riina often says that one must never kill a *cristiano*, which in Italian means both "Christian" and "human being," yet he turns around and does exactly that. Riina sees himself as a larger-than-life figure, resorting to omertà to justify his actions, alluding cleverly to the historical plight of Sicilians by suggestion. As John Lawrence Reynolds notes, it is in such subtle ways that the code imbues the Mafia with a sense of self-dignity and historical validation, since omertà "was born not from the machinations of a criminal mastermind but out of the desperate necessity of middle-class Sicilian families seeking control over their lives," and this makes it possible to see that the "appalling behavior of the Mafia and its various progeny is actually rooted in good intentions."[17] This theme is implicit in many early movies on the Mafia, including *Italian Blood* (1911), *Omertà* (1912), *Dramma alla masseria* (1912), *The Padrone's Ward* (1914), *Tresa* (1915), and *Malacarne* (1918).

The appeal of omertà can be explained, in part, in psychological terms. The code is appealing because it embraces an archetypal view of manliness and masculinity that is present in folk legends worldwide. It can be called the "Robin Hood archetype" mixed in with the "Shadow archetype," as Carl Jung calls it—the archetype that expresses people's innate fear of the dark and of secret or mysterious ongoings.[18] Mafia culture is both Robin Hood and Shadow culture. This is why Mafiosi link themselves to pirates, famous historical bandits, and the like. A case

in point is that of the legendary bandit Salvatore Giuliano, which merits
some commentary here, since he was the most famous bandit in Italian
history, rising to the level of a folk hero, in large part because Giuliano
understood the power of the media. The image of Giuliano as a rugged
and handsome "bad boy" and Robin Hood figure was captured by the
cameras, bestowing iconic power on him, as Dickie notes, writing the
following:

> At the peak of his notoriety, Salvatore Giuliano made himself as
> accessible for photojournalists as he was elusive for the authorities.
> Consequently, his features are still instantly recognizable in Italy. In
> one of the most familiar photographs, he looks straight into the cam-
> era, his thumbs hooked inside the belt from which his holster hangs,
> his jacket pushed behind his hips to reveal a loose shirt unbuttoned
> at the neck. Giuliano had what is called an open countenance. By a
> recent calculation, forty-one biographies of him have been written
> since his death—more than any other person in postwar Italian histo-
> ry. Each book has promised finally to reveal the secrets hidden be-
> hind that broad, handsome face.[19]

Giuliano's reign as Italy's Robin Hood lasted from 1943 to 1950. He
prevailed for such an extensive period of time because he was protected
opportunistically by the Mafia in collusion with corrupt politicians.
When he was no longer useful to them, they murdered him. He became
famous because he knew how to manipulate the media, writing letters
to newspapers and giving interviews to journalists. He was photogenic
and young—the perfect image of a swashbuckling folk hero. Admired
by peasants and portraying himself as a staunch anti-communist, he
became a veritable icon in his heyday. As support for Giuliano began to
fade, he was shot dead by his close friend, Gaspare Pisciotta, purportedly under coercion by the Mafia.

Many Mafiosi came to model themselves after Giuliano. The idea
that gangsters are fashionable and handsome, yet brutal, has its own
charm.[20] They belong to that "forbidden universe," as previously mentioned, that common people seem unwilling to enter into, to escape the
banality of modern living.[21] As Bill James writes, gangster archetypes
are appealing to Americans because they are part of a morality tale from
which they can learn something about themselves,[22] being "an expression of our impulse to draw a protective circle around ourselves."[23] But

lost in all this mythic glorification of criminals is, ultimately, the intense human suffering that comes from their crimes. Demystifying the archetype and the symbolism is crucial in bringing about a change in this deeply rooted attitude.

As Reynolds observes, the Mafia likes to tell archetypal stories of early bandits who showed uncommon courage, the most famous of whom was a man named Saponara, captured and imprisoned by Spanish invaders in 1578:

> According to Sicilian lore, Saponara was tortured by his Spanish captors in an effort to learn the names of his cohorts, but Saponara chose to die in agony rather than betray others. His bravery became a symbol for every Sicilian who believed their salvation could be achieved only through loyalty. [24]

But reality is vastly different from the legends. The real Mafia boss is not a larger-than-life personage, as is Marlon Brando in *The Godfather*. He is a brutal killer whose deeds are not romanticized by the gripping music of Nino Rota. No one says to a real capo, "Leave the gun; take the cannoli," as in the movie. The Mafia loves to romanticize its image. In fact, the notion of *padrino* (godfather) comes from the movie, not from real Mafia culture. It is a convenient fiction that the Mafia has willingly adopted from the silver screen. The reason for this, nevertheless, makes historical sense. The *padrino* figure is, actually, an ancient archetype in Mediterranean cultures. His role is seen as a means for reinforcing family cohesiveness. He is a backup plan for fatherhood (should the biological father disappear from the family either through death or by wandering). All secret organizations, including noncriminal ones, have a *padrino*, or kingpin figurehead, who is in charge. In southern Italian religious culture, the *padrino* is perceived as being more important to preserving family unity than the biological father. He is seen to be a kind of wise elder, providing sustenance to the family, both material and moral. The "capo-as-padrino," as mentioned earlier, was adopted by the Mafia from *The Godfather*, seeing to it that it quickly became part of its own pseudo-religious mythology. Real *padrini* do not resemble the *padrini* of Hollywood. They appear commonplace, often rough looking and unassuming. To moviegoing audiences, images of real-life Mafiosi are thus somewhat jarring.

All this collage of archetypes and myths would not have been possible in the first place without a sustaining code of omertà. The code allows Mafiosi to claim manly honor, in contradistinction to common hoods. Unlike the latter, the Mafia formalizes and thus legitimizes its vendettas, using its own form of tribunal justice reminiscent of the Inquisition, with similar interrogation techniques and ferocious punishments against both nonpaying individuals of the *pizzo* and internal traitors (those who betray the Mob by either leaving it or going to the authorities). The *faccia tagliata* ("the cut face"), for instance, is an indelible sign of infamy among the mobsters; it derives from the same kind of punishment meted out by the inquisitors to heretics. The "stone in the mouth" is also reminiscent of Inquisition symbolism, constituting a version of the *mordacchia* (a type of muzzle) used by the inquisitors to punish blasphemers. The testimony of a certain Salvatore D'Amico in the 1870s before a judge in Sicily accusing certain Mafiosi for having murdered his two sons dramatically emphasizes what Mafia justice is all about: "I will die at the hands of the Mafia because without doubt I will be killed. Neither you yourself, your authority, or the entire police force will be able to save me. A mother never forgives her dishonorable children" (translation ours).[25]

Eleven days after giving this testimony, D'Amico was found shot dead with a *tappo* ("cork") in his mouth. The message was clear—from the mouth of a dishonorable man nothing should come out, not even his bad breath. Other symbols are the cut hand left on the chest, which denotes that the victim had stolen from an area that was under the control of the Mafia, and the genitals hanging around the neck to indicate that the victim had attempted to seduce the woman of a Mafioso while the latter was in jail.

The Camorra constitutes an exception to all this, since it appears not to have any discernable code of honor, other than espousing some basic principles that go back considerably in time (1842) to a code called *il frieno*, which it abandoned. It does not have an initiation ceremony. Its activities are rarely covert, probably because the Camorra deals primarily in contraband and thus needs members to play visible roles in criminal operations. Another major difference is the way in which the Camorra discourages rigid hierarchical structure. As Shelley Klein notes, this is an advantage because it is "very difficult for opposition groups to eradicate any particular Camorra 'family,' for without a recognizable head of operations and subordinate chiefs, there are no targets."[26]

## THE POWER OF THE CODE

The main way in which the Mafia conducts its extortion operations is by demanding a percentage of a victim's earnings or a fixed rate from businesses in exchange for protection. Simple demand for money would be perceived as being undignified and a vulgar form of street crime. In this way, a kind of "honorable system of taxation" is set up and used to justify the intimidation and violence to be used if failure to pay emerges as a possibility. This is, clearly, a clever tactic for ennobling a criminal enterprise. It bespeaks of honor, not vulgarity. By extorting common citizens in this way, the Mafia is better able to establish a firm control over its territories, assuming taxation authority properly belonging to the government. Surveys show that a majority of commercial businesses in Sicily and other parts of Italy submit to the *pizzo* willingly. Along with the code of silence—both as a system for maintaining control over members within the Mafia and a threat of reprisal for anyone who runs to the authorities—this type of *pizzo* racket works effectively and efficiently. Those who are being extorted prefer not to make a fuss, agreeing to pay the "reasonable" *pizzo* as part of the expense of running a business. They often choose to risk criminal charges of perjury or false testimony rather than to risk the wrath of reprisal from their extortionists.

As Lunde notes, this form of extortion racketeering is the basis of both real-life Mafia activities and, of course, gangster movies, and it was the activity that installed the Mafia permanently into American society. Here's how it took place:

> In the 19th century, an organization that helped newly arrived Italians in the United States to find homes and work was the Unione Siciliana, which had branches across the country. It was infiltrated by extortionists, the so-called "Black Hand gang," the foremost of whom was Ignazio Saietta. By 1901, Saietta had become the national chairman of the Unione Siciliana, and he filled its regional offices with many of his criminal associates. Many new Italian immigrants, especially in New York, were leaned on to pay a percentage of their

weekly wage to the extortionists, fearing violence and the loss of their jobs. Small businesses such as grocers, drug stores, and barbers also paid "protection."[27]

The anti-Mafia movement that sporadically surfaces in Sicily and Calabria is appropriately termed *Addiopizzo* ("Goodbye to the *Pizzo*"), implying that if one breaks the code of silence and does not collaborate by paying the *pizzo*, the Mafia will be defeated. But this is easier said than done, given the power of the silence code. The *pizzo* phenomenon penetrates deeply into the fabric of Sicilian and Calabrian culture and the mind-set of those growing up in such a culture, spreading to other parts of contemporary Italy. Being the wise guys that they are, the Mafiosi are extremely careful not to drive their victims to bankruptcy. Too much greed is seen as being counterproductive and "immoral," tending to injudiciously provoke a public outcry, not to mention public pressure on the police to intervene. Gouging victims is simply not good for business, especially since the extortion business is easy to prosecute in the courts. However, as new technologies surface faster than regulating laws, the opportunities in cyberspace seem literally infinite for mobsters, as Lunde observes: "Organized criminals are now able to carry out protection rackets without moving from their desks."[28]

Anthropologists divide the main spheres of culture into basic domains and their attendant institutions—kinship, religion, politics, law, economics, and education. These generate consensus and guarantee general adherence to the norms of behavior and communication that are deemed appropriate by the collectivity as a whole. These are established and enforced primarily by those who are centrally located within the most dominant sphere at a specific point in time. If that sphere is the religious one, for instance, then the leader or leaders of that sphere will dictate what the norms are; if it is the secular political sphere, then those located in a central position within that sphere will determine them. Those who do not comply with such norms risk censure, punishment, or marginalization. Indeed, those who reject them outright must show the validity of why they are doing so publicly. Otherwise, they risk facing some form of castigation.

The Mafia system is a small-scale model of basic culture. In fact, it is made up of an extended kinship sphere, as previously discussed. It also espouses its own forms of religion, politics, law, and education. Coalescing into the code of omertà, the syndicate can maintain an ideal of manliness, honor, and respect, imbuing it with historical validity by tracing it back to the era when Sicily was ruled by despots. It is both subversive and compelling, since it offers an alternative to ineffectual and corrupt systems of government. But unlike civil institutions, the fundamental principle of justice espoused by Mafia culture is the vendetta; however, as already mentioned, vendettas cannot be carried out in the form of brutal revenges. They are to be carried out according to the norms of respect and honor as spelled out by the code of omertà. In personal quarrels, for example, a Mafioso must show aplomb and control as he takes the law into his own hands, gaining the upper hand through poised enactments of violence. And, of course, Mafiosi must look out for one another in all situations. Any offense against an individual Mafioso or the Mafia clan will trigger a vendetta campaign by the Mafioso's partners.

The vendetta resonates with a biblical "eye for an eye" meaning. An established form of justice in many rural cultures to this day, the vendetta serves to punish crimes wherever governments are greatly distrusted. In the case of a blood feud, the clan of the murdered individual must seek vengeance on the murderer or on the killer's family. No wonder that Hollywood and the media have become enraptured by this concept of vendetta, with movies using the term as a title proliferating, from a 1919 German film entitled *Vendetta* to the 2006 film *V for Vendetta*. Vendetta, silence, and honor all converge in the code of omertà, imbuing it with great emotional resonance.

Deadly vendetta warfare among Mafia clans is a common occurrence as they vie for territorial hegemony to carry out their criminal activities and, more importantly, lay a geographical stake to establish their pseudo-statehood. The threat of punishment in no way deters Mafiosi from their activities and lifestyle; in fact, it fuels it. Membership in a clan is perceived as prestigious and even an obligatory coming-of-age rite for many young people in Sicily, Calabria, Naples, and many American inner-city districts. The enormous emotional appeal of omertà, with its manly and religious symbolism, probably has much more to do with the continuing appeal of the Mafia today than many might think.[29] Glorified by movies, gang warfare affords many young people the opportunity to become empowered and feel the sheltering effect of the Mob.[30]

Historically, in Sicily, the territory claimed by a clan was called a *cosca*. In Sicilian, a *cosca* refers to the heart of an artichoke (its middle stem), which is protected by the surrounding leaves of the plant, which are often thorny. The *cosca* thus perfectly symbolizes the fact that the Mafia is sheltered or protected from outside forces. The appearance of these *cosche* was due, in part, to existing social conditions (as mentioned in the previous chapter) and the *cosca*'s alliance with some revolutionary cause aiming to bring about political or social change, for instance, Italian Unification. For a *cosca* to gain a foothold in the social terrain, it required leadership and structure. The leader came to be called a *capocosca*, and he was expected to be a prominent figure in the social milieu where the *cosca* was located. He could be a nobleman, a *gabellotto* (someone who leased land from the aristocrats), a well-known person, or even a priest with revolutionary inclinations. Many villages or neighborhoods had a *cosca*. It offered real protection against various corrupt forces in the society.

But near the end of the nineteenth century, the *cosche* started becoming less and less tied to some social cause and more and more inclined to enact their own style of justice. As they began losing their original function, they started gradually being taken over by small tightly knit groups of criminals, whose purpose was hardly to bring about social change, but to ensure personal financial gain. They continued to present themselves as an alternative form of justice to the corrupt legal system, even though they acted in blatant self-interest, gaining power and control through extortion activities. Nevertheless, the new *cosche* were perceived as constituting parallel justice systems and even self-contained economic systems, becoming, in many regions of Sicily, the de facto authority structures. Agriculture, for instance, was the main economic activity of the Corleone *cosca*, commerce of the Palermo *cosca*, and fishing of the Castellammare del Golfo *cosca*. Each *capocosca* gained prominence by corrupting public officials through intimidation and bribery. Seeing what was occurring, law-abiding citizens had no choice but to resort to a *cosca* for protection, thus living in two juridical universes, and paying taxes to both—to the legally constituted government of the region and to the *cosca*. In return, the *cosca* offered assurance that they would not harm a business or a specific person, although they claimed to also protect the business or individual from common street criminals and corrupt authorities (if need be). As a common Sicilian proverb aptly puts it, *A paura guarda a vigna, no a sipala*, which means, "It is fear that oversees a vinyard, not a fence." The *lupara*, the sawed-off shotgun used by *cosca* members, became the symbol of vendetta justice. Today, any powerful weapon will do the job.

The original foot soldiers of the *capocosca*, known as the *picciotti* ("little ones"), were coopted enforcers who shared the booty with him. To ensure that the *cosca* maintained a separate identity from common street criminals, the code of omertà was enforced, demanding that any-one who cheated was to be punished and ensuring that loyalty to the *cosca* was maintained through brutal enforcement. At first, this ren-dered the internal cohesion of a *cosca* fragile, since disputes and jeal-ousies were common and resolved through bloodshed. Vying for territo-ry and dominance among the various *cosche* was also commonplace. But territorial disputes gradually resolved themselves in the service of self-interest for everyone concerned, and the code of omertà allowed for the *cosche* to survive outside threats. Silence emerged as the com-mon language of the *cosche*. Talk was replaced by a powerful body language, for instance, the dire-looking face and the gesture of cutting someone's throat or face, becoming part of a system of terror and con-trol. "The best word is the one not spoken" was, and continues to be, a basic commandment of the omertà code.

The *padrino*, as already touched upon, is a Hollywood invention. In the actual Sicilian Mafia, no such figure existed before *The Godfather*. The boss could, of course, have been a godfather to someone in the *cosca*, but it was not a requirement. Nevertheless, the notion of a leader as a godfather fits in perfectly with general *padrino* culture in southern Italy. There was, however, a *parrina* in real Mafia culture, a kind of bordello madam—the term being a distortion of the *madrina* ("god-mother") figure into a provider of sexual entertainment for the Mafiosi. The *parrinu* was the local parish priest, and the *parrineddu* was writer Leonardo Sciascia's portrayal of a pathetic figure who "talked too much."

The Mafia's welcoming of the *padrino* figure into its symbolic uni-verse is a convenient fiction that adds to ensconcing its mythology. This event is a perfect example of the power of what the late French philoso-pher Jean Baudrillard called the simulacrum, a state of mind whereby the world of fiction is perceived as being more real than reality—a state that he called hyperreality.[31] From early myths to legends told about heroes, real and fictitious, we seem to prefer living in the realm of fantasy over real life. The borderline between fiction and reality breaks down through the power of symbolism. And our myths and legends have always been hyperreal, that is, perceived as larger than life, and thus as more real than real. The cinematic *padrino* is a Hollywood simulacrum, penetrating real Mafia culture.

## MAFIA WOMEN

The Mafia is a patriarchal organization. Like most criminal gangs, it is a testosterone-driven enterprise, espousing tacit principles of pseudo-masculinity. Originally, women were called *panza lenta* ("loose guts") because they were seen as being too talkative and gossipy and thus "spilling their guts out." Men, on the other hand, were called *uomini di panza* ("men of the gut") because they could be trusted not to talk and spill the beans. Ironically, it was the men who, as *pentiti* in the 1980s and 1990s, talked willingly to the authorities. By and large, women are perceived to be supplementary role players by the Mob, even though today female liberation has made some inroads into Mafia culture, with women showing themselves to be as violent as their male counter-parts.[32] Omertà has, however, always assigned subservient roles to the women, even though the wives of modern-day *capi* might be expected to run the affairs of the clan behind the scenes, if necessary. In other criminal groups, like the Mexican cartel, the wife will often take over the "family business" if the husband is either jailed or killed.

There is a history of active participation of women in the 'Ndranghe-ta, which has an extended family structure that is totally dependent upon women to carry out traditional family roles. In effect, in the *'ndrine*, the criminal and extended "families" are one and the same, and the women in them assume roles according to a hierarchy of power mirroring the actual hierarchy in the clan—the wife of a capo is more powerful among women than is the wife of a foot soldier, for example. She is expected to ensure that her husband's reputation is maintained. There are documented examples of young 'Ndrangheta girls who, hav-ing fallen in love with a *carabiniere* ("policeman"), ended up being killed by her family for a *questione d'onore* ("a point of honor"). Flirta-tion or adultery with other men are not tolerated on any level. Essentially, 'Ndrangheta men are expected to "marry the sisters and daughters of other men of honor," writes Dickie, or "women who have lived in a mafia environment all their lives and are therefore more likely to have the kind of discretion and/or submissiveness that the organization requires of them."[33] Arranged marriages are common and form the basis for expanding the power of a family.

Although seen as subservient, the women are held in high respect, and they are expected to follow a strict moral code, but when it comes to the men, a double standard surfaces. Mistresses are tolerated as part of manliness, although they are to be kept secret. Brazen and open sexual shenanigans of any type are strictly forbidden, but extramarital sex for the men is not only tolerated, but in some instances even encouraged. At no time, however, must the affair come out into the open. Cawthorne and Cawthorne tell a story related to Brooklyn mobster Frankie Saggio, born in 1964, which brings this out emphatically:

> From the age of seven, his uncle would take him over the East River to have a haircut, a shoeshine, and a lunch in Little Italy. It was there that Frankie got a detailed education in the ways of Cosa Nostra. Uncle Philly was steeped in the Mafia ethos. His father-in-law was Carlo Gambino, head of the Gambino crime family. If one of his men turned up at his house with his girlfriend, the door would be shut in his face. He would be told to come with his wife, or not at all.[34]

Promiscuity for the men is seen as actually preserving family unity since the implicit principle of the code is that "boys will be boys." Mafia men have mistresses, as men of power and influence often do. On the other hand, if the women are caught in an adulterous relation, they are banished from the family or punished in sometimes brutal ways. Omertà is certainly a convenient code for Mafia men; not so much for the women. As Reynolds observes, "Any woman who swears risks being labeled a *puttana*, a prostitute, and cheating on a husband who happens to be a 'made' man is a capital crime."[35] This view of sexual relations is consistent with patriarchal cultures and, in Europe, has a tradition that goes as far back as the Renaissance (and perhaps even before). It is evident, for instance, in the plays of Calderón, the Spanish dramatist and poet, who was the last prominent figure of the golden age. The main theme of his writing is the exaltation of the Castilian code of honor requiring husband, father, or brother to punish the transgressions of an unfaithful woman.

Despite the double standard, there is nonetheless a deep-seated respect for women that derives more from general Sicilian culture than it does from the code of omertà. Moreover, the situation is changing. The growing importance of women in the modern Mafia and 'Ndrangheta is no doubt a consequence of the progressive liberation of women from their traditional housewife roles in Italian society. In the past, the women were more likely to stay in their place, and their influence, which was indirect or suggestive, did not extend beyond the husband or the immediate home environment. In the 'Ndrangheta, only if a woman showed particular criminal qualities could she rise to be a *sorella* ("sister") *d'omertà*. This honor, however, was not, and still is not, open to any woman. It is restricted to a wife, daughter, sister, or fiancée of a clan male who shows prowess in criminality. There are documented cases of Mafia and 'Ndrangheta women seeking to avenge some perceived wrong by imploring the men of the clan to track down and eliminate the wrongdoer or even taking the vendetta into their own hands.

So, in some ways, Mafia and 'Ndrangheta wives are hardly the silent homebodies of traditional Sicilian and Calabrian culture. They have always helped their men run Mob affairs, at least behind the scenes.[36] The 'Ndrangheta, in particular, relies on women to ensure that secrecy is maintained throughout the family system. Together with its rule of restricted membership, this role of women provides a lasting and solid structure to the criminal organization, which makes an *'ndrina* difficult to penetrate and defeat. Calabrians are less likely to inform on their criminal colleagues with whom they have familial bonds. Overseeing this code of secrecy is the *femmina* (*himmena* in Calabrian), who ensures that its strictures are maintained and respected within the fold. In the case of imprisoned husbands, the women become valuable liaisons or conduits between the husbands and the other members. On the other hand, *'ndrina* women have also been instrumental in provoking clan feuds, which can result in lost territory and the disruption of family units. In such cases, the women cannot remain passive, because a threat to the clan implies a threat to the family.

But ultimately, life in a criminal family is alienating for many women, especially young ones. Growing up in such a family isolates them from the rest of society. A young Mafia woman tends not to have any contact of any meaningful duration with individuals outside her family. She also is prohibited from interacting with, or frequenting, "certain persons." If she does, she will invariably have to pay the price. There are many documented cases of Mafia and 'ndrina young women being murdered and left to rot on the streets for the dishonor they have brought to the family through their relationships with outsiders.

As Schneider and Schneider have written, the role of women in the Mafia is thus paradoxical; it is both empowering and enslaving.[37] The practice of violence, according to the code of honor, being a pseudo-chivalric one, generally excludes women from the exercise and display of violence. Women are perceived to be the beneficiaries of the criminal lifestyle, not participants in it. A Mafia wife is expected to be an aristocratic woman. She hosts her husband's friends, while basking in the refined lifestyle that money and status bring. The Mafia looks out for its women, punishing those who "fool around" with them. The love of their men means a lot to many of the women, who sense that they are getting much more romantic attention than they would otherwise get. Omertà is attractive to some women, who are fascinated by its secret lifestyle, with its macho men and the prospect of immense wealth. It is what draws them to, and keeps them in, the fold, even though, as Reynolds astutely observes, they are well aware of the double standard:

> The benefits include the prospect that her man will rise high enough in the ranks to generate an impressive flow of income, permitting her and her family to enjoy the perks of wealth—a large home, expensive clothes, luxury cars, and first-class vacations. Another perk is respect from her husband and his cohorts. The family remains a powerful unifying force among Sicilians and especially among Cosa Nostra members. You don't embarrass your wife, and you don't abuse her either.[38]

Living on the edge seems to be romantically engaging. The criminal lifestyle is exciting because it is dangerous, and danger, as the great German philosopher Friedrich Nietzsche so aptly phrased it, is the "greatest fruitfulness and the greatest enjoyment of existence."[39] The promise of romance, protection, respect, and excitement is very attractive, at least at a subconscious level. The sexuality of the "bad boy" is the stuff of legend, but there is a price to pay. The women have to accept the fact that the manliness code of omertà not only allows the men to be promiscuous, it implicitly demands it, since a wise guy "who is without a mistress or two may be suspect."[40] Weekdays are for wives; weekends are for mistresses. This tacit rule is understood by both the men and women, ensuring that there are no risks of embarrassments. It is part of the code of silence. However, the code is often counterproductive and even dangerous for the Mafiosi themselves. Tales of lurid sexuality and consequent internal vendettas abound in Mafia history. It is written that one of the most famous Cosa Nostra bosses of all time, Vito Genovese, had another Mafioso killed because he lusted after his wife. The murder was rationalized as an act of passion. Clearly, the rules of omertà can conveniently be set aside if need be.

Furthermore, the code of manliness demands complete avoidance of homosexuality, as the case of John ("Johnny Boy") D'Amato so brutally brings out. Reynolds summarizes it as follows:

> D'Amato was head of the DeCavalcante family, the largest in New Jersey and reputed to be the basis of the popular *The Sopranos* television series. He had also been a confidante of the notorious John Gotti, a relationship that might have protected him in other times and other circumstances. With his girlfriend Kelly, D'Amato began frequenting clubs where men and women swapped partners and engaged in group sex. At more than one of these events, D'Amato's girlfriend witnessed him performing oral sex on other men, and she tearfully confessed it to one of D'Amato's wise guy friends. When the friend reported the incident to Mafia heavyweight Vincent (Vinnie Ocean) Palermo, the mob boss ordered D'Amato's murder. The motive was clear. "Nobody's gonna respect us if we have a gay homosexual boss sitting down discussing business," D'Amato's killer testified in court.[41]

An unwritten commandment of the omertà code is that, if you are a Mafia man, you can have all the sex you want, discretely, as long as it is heterosexual. In 1902, the Calabrian police found a document containing rules for admission into the 'Ndrangheta in which it is explicitly stated that homosexuals were prohibited from joining. Male chauvinism seems to be alive and well among criminal secret societies. Ironically, however, in a 2009 trial, a Gambino family *pentito* admitted that he was gay, living in the closet for many years. He did this as a gambit to obtain a more lenient sentence for a crime he had committed in 2003.

Lost in all this self-serving concoction of pseudo-chivalric notions is the brutality that underpins the criminal lifestyle. In reality, being married to, or the mistress of, a mobster is hardly a matter of exciting romance, with stylish clothing and cosmetics, as the movies and television programs proclaim. The glamorous fantasy that is created both by Mafia fiction and Hollywood fiction is just that—fantasy.

## THE YAKUZA

It is interesting, at this point, to make a comparison between the Italian criminal organizations and the Japanese Yakuza, given that there are striking parallels between the two.[42] The Yakuza constitutes one of the largest organized crime syndicates in the world today. In Japan, as of 2005, there were nearly 90,000 known members, eclipsed only by Hong Kong's Triads, with 160,000 members.[43]

Japanese society places great value on conformity. A common Japanese proverb states, "The nail that sticks up must be hammered down." Individualism generates suspicion, but acts of individualism inspire silent admiration. This is why the Yakuza, which stubbornly refuses to fit into the traditional Japanese social mold, have secret admirers among the Japanese populace. The origin of the gang is traced to the early seventeenth century, when a group of "crazy men," called the *kabuki-mono*, purportedly engaged in criminal activities, standing out through odd clothing styles, bizarre haircuts, and violent behavior, which involved the use of long swords. The *kabuki-mono* harassed and terrorized those living in their immediate milieu. They would use their swords to literally cut down anyone who went against them or even for the sheer pleasure of it. They also spoke a self-made slang, so that no one could listen in on their plans. They swore absolute loyalty to one another, protecting one another no matter what the circumstances, even going against their own families, if necessary. Having no established system of leadership, they eventually lost their ability to control people and thus started to wander nomadically around Japan as a band of thugs, pillaging villages and towns. Many historians believe that the Yakuza descended from this band of gangster-warriors.

The Yakuza, however, denies any historical linkage to the *kabuki-mono*. Like the Mafia, they spin a different tale of their origins, linking themselves to groups of brave individuals (storekeepers, tavern owners) known as the *machi-yakko*, who took up arms against criminals, including the *kabuki-mono*, in defense of their towns and villages. They were common people and purported to be skillful gamblers. The term *Yakuza* derives from the Japanese words for "eight + nine + three," referring to the worst hand in a gambling game. The group established a chain of command, much like today's Yakuza, and developed various symbols and rituals to set themselves apart from other gangs, garnering the support of the people in their crusade against common street thugs. According to legend, they had few weapons, using their bare hands and pugilistic skills to vanquish their opponents. They rose to folk hero status in a short period time. Their exploits have been extolled and magnified in legends, stories, and plays about them. "Yakuza leaders," notes Lunde, "have devised largely mythological genealogies linking themselves to these past folk heroes."[44] But the evidence for this is slim at best, specious at worst.

Like the Mafia, the Yakuza see their ancestry in chivalric traditions. They think of themselves as *ronin*, "masterless men," in the tradition of the samurai warriors of the past. The samurai were members of a hereditary warrior class who defended the estates of aristocrats. They wore a distinctive helmet and armor and used two curved swords, one long and one short. They became folk heroes throughout Japan. Many see the Yakuza as their descendants. For this reason, much of its criminal activities are overlooked by the populace at large, which is beguiled by the tattoos, martial arts skills, and power of the samurai code of honor. But when one demystifies the group's origins and its code of honor, the Yakuza, like the Mafia, are nothing but ruthless criminals who seek power and wealth through intimidation and violence.

Yakuza membership is not through bloodlines. Those who join tend to be from poorer backgrounds or are social misfits. The Yakuza clan functions as their adoptive family, providing them with a sense of belonging to something meaningful. Each new member must pledge loyalty to the code and the other members. The Yakuza unit has a "godfather" at the top, with new members initiated into the fold through a ceremony and assigned to a lower position in a pyramidal structure. The initiates are conceived as "children," and the term used to designate their relation to the head is *oyabun-kobun*, which translates as "father-child," mimicking the samurai warrior's allegiance to his feudal over-lord. As Kaplan and Dubro put it, "The *oyabun* provides advice, protection, and help, and in return receives the unswerving loyalty and service of his *kobun* when needed."[45] Initiation rites are highly formal, including an exchange of *saké* cups (a traditional rice alcoholic drink) to symbolize the exchange of blood between the *oyabun* and the *kobun*. The ceremony is carried out in a Shinto shrine, which imbues it with religious undertones.

While the venue, the circumstances, and the culture may be different, it is obvious that the Mafia and the Yakuza share many of the same formalisms (or, more accurately, delusions). Blood symbolism is crucial to both. A candidate for admission into the Mafia must participate in a ceremony in which his trigger finger is pricked and the resulting blood smeared on the image of a saint. The picture is then set on fire, burning the initiate's hands as he swears his loyalty and silent obedience to the family. Blood is not exchanged in the Yakuza ceremony, but *saké* is, as mentioned, which is a metaphorical substitute and connected to a life-giving substance in Japan—rice.

Like the Mafia, the basis of Yakuza operations is extortion but also includes smuggling, prostitution, drug-dealing, and gambling. And like their Mafia counterparts, the Yakuza control restaurants and trucking companies. In the 1980s, they also engaged in real estate speculation. In recent years, the Yakuza have been forced to change their recruitment standards. Most new members come from the *bosozoku*, the name for violent street punks, who ride proudly and arrogantly around in motor-cycles. The Yakuza who treasure their ancestral forms of recruitment reject the recruits, considering them an insult to the dignified mettle of the group. But the world is changing for the Yakuza, as it is for the Mafia.

The Yakuza is an exclusive male society. They do not trust women, seeing them as weaklings and thus as a threat to their organization. The only woman who is expected to play any role at all in the gang is the leader's wife, called *ane-san*, meaning "older sister." She is given the same respect as the boss, simply because she is his wife. Unlike 'Ndrangheta and Mafia women, however, she is not allowed get involved in any of the criminal enterprises or to give advice of any kind. To a Yakuza member, the most important personality trait is courage, which women are thought to lack. If there is a conflict, the Yakuza warrior must be ready to fight to the death. Women are mothers and wives, not warriors. The Yakuza believe that they should stay at home and look after the children, not engage in men's affairs. In this way, they will not have access to information and thus cannot talk to the authorities.

The Yakuza have elaborate initiation rituals, which include the application of elaborate tattoos covering the entire torso, as well the arms and legs.[46] Naked, a Yakuza looks like a painted mural, with images of dragons, flowers, landscapes, and gang insignias. The new member is supposed to show his determination and courage by subjecting himself to hundreds of hours of painful tattooing. Like the Mafia, the Yakuza enforces loyalty to the clan by using vendettas against anyone seen as being disloyal or any member who tries to distance himself from the gang. A Yakuza who offends or fails to execute some assignment will have his finger cut off at a joint (*yubitsume*) and must then present it to the boss—a practice highlighted in the first *Kill Bill* film by director Quentin Tarantino. For serious acts of disloyalty, the offending Yakuza is given the choice of committing "honorable suicide" or being killed by his confreres.

As stated, the Yakuza power structure is pyramidal, with a boss, the *oyabun*, on top and loyal underlings, the *kobun*, beneath him. When a new recruit is accepted into the Yakuza, he must vow his allegiance, loyalty, obedience, and duty to the *oyabun*, who, like a father, is supposed to provide protection and good advice to him. There is also a *kumicho* ("supreme boss"), a *saiko komon* ("senior adviser"), and a *so-honbucho* ("headquarters manager"). The *wakagashira* ("number-two man") is equivalent to the Mafia underboss and is responsible for overseeing the operations of various gangs. He is aided by the *fuku-honbucho*, who is responsible for several gangs of his own. A typical Yakuza family will also have dozens of *shatei* ("younger brothers") and many *wakashu* ("junior leaders").

Like the Mafia, the staying power of the Yakuza involves funneling funds obtained by crime into legitimate businesses, as Lunde points out, writing the following:

> Organized crime is an economic activity and differs from street gangs like the Bloods and Crips, not just in the degree of organization and purpose, but because organized crime accumulates capital and reinvests it. It is this that differentiates organized criminal groups from

street gangs and "unorganized" criminals. It is the accumulated capital of organized groups like the U.S. Mafia and the Yakuza that enables them to buy the political protection that allows them to diversify and to respond to market shifts, such as the upsurge in demand for illicit drugs in the 1980s and human trafficking in the 1990s.[47]

The Yakuza are glorified in film. The 1974 film entitled simply *The Yakuza* reinforces the legend of the Yakuza as originating to protect poor people in small towns from traveling bands of marauding noblemen, adopting a code of honor as rigorous as the samurai code of Bushido. The claim is also made that the Yakuza disallow membership to foreigners. In Tarantino's *Kill Bill*, there is a scene that shows the Yakuza bosses of five families as being upset that a "Chinese-Japanese half-breed" woman named O-Ren has become a boss several years after killing the former head of the family. One of the male bosses exclaims that this is an outrage for the "fathers of the fathers, of the fathers, of the fathers of the men sitting here [who] started this."

In the end, the Yakuza are, like the Mafia, part self-styled fiction and part media fiction. Like their Italian counterparts, they are gaining strength and power because of this "dual fictionalizing" process. They are even migrating to other countries and have become heavily involved in cybercrime. But the global cyber-village is also allowing common people to fight back. There are signs that the Yakuza's lure is diminishing, as Japanese citizens, like the *Addiopizzo* members in Sicily, are fighting back by writing blogs against them and encouraging opposition through social media. But these signs can be deceiving, since Japanese youth, like Italian and American youth, are still drawn to a group where a sense of belonging, along with honor and respect, can be achieved through trials of bravery. Because they are tightly knit as a group and secretive in their lifestyles and criminal operations, like the fabled ninjas of ancient Japan, the Yakuza can be everywhere and nowhere. They terrorize by their silence. And they remain lethal.

# 3

# RITUALS AND SYMBOLS

You never see animals going through the absurd and often horrible fooleries of magic and religion. Dogs do not ritually urinate in the hope of persuading heaven to do the same and send down rain. Asses do not bray a liturgy to cloudless skies. Nor do cats attempt, by abstinence from cat's meat, to wheedle the feline spirits into benevolence. Only man behaves with such gratuitous folly. It is the price he has to pay for being intelligent but not, as yet, quite intelligent enough.

—Aldous Huxley (1894–1963)

*The Godfather, Part III* revolves around the Mafia's involvement with, and connection to, the Catholic Church, bringing out the fact that the Mafia sees itself, or at least portrays itself, as a quasi-religious institution. At a social event in the movie, the character Michael Corleone is seen donating $100 million "to the poor of Sicily," which he gives to the Church to distribute equitably. The implication is that the Mafia is an honorable and charitable organization that traces its own roots, ipso facto, to groups of valiant men whose intention has always been to help the poor—in line with the myth of *cavalleria rusticana*. Religion is a frequent theme in *The Sopranos*. In episode 9 of the second season, for example, a mobster is shot and pronounced dead for approximately one minute, during which time he has a chilling vision of hell. This makes another mobster nervous, because he is very superstitious. So he goes to a priest asking him if donations to the church would be enough for forgiveness for a life of brutality so that he can escape the fires of damnation. Mobsters may not have a conscience, but they certainly do understand that their actions are profoundly immoral and evil. And like everyone else, they fear retribution.

The use of religious symbols and rituals in Mafia initiation rites imparts a pseudo-spiritual authority to the Mafia. Joining the Mafia is akin to joining a religious order, complete with oaths, rituals, special symbolic practices, rules of conduct, punishments, and so on. Omertà is as much a self-styled religious code as it is a pseudo-chivalric one. This connection to religion, fictive (through the use of imitative symbols and rituals) and nonfictive (through actual adherence to real religious practices), allows the Mafia, the 'Ndrangheta, and other criminal organizations to insert themselves seamlessly into the religious cultural substratum of southern Italy. This is seen in the *Godfather* films, as well as in the HBO series *The Sopranos*, with the many trips to Italy and to churches that American mobsters take in various episodes. In the movies and real life, the tradition of churchgoing is part of the code of omertà. There is one reference in the second *Godfather* movie to the Mafia being a 2,000-year-old Italian secret religious society. This is, of course, fiction, but it is a convenient fiction for the real Mafia, allowing it to create a mystique for itself shrouded in mystery. A parallel claim is seen in the film *The Yakuza*, which represents the actual claims of the Yakuza. The movie opens by informing the viewer that the Yakuza have been in Japan for more than 350 years, abiding by a code of honor as rigorous as the samurai code of Bushido.

Rituals and symbolism are what give claims like these permanence and significance. Without them, the criminal organizations would have a harder time maintaining the crucial emotional bonds among their members that keep them intact. They are means for ensuring continuity. One of the most important ceremonies for criminal groups is the one used for initiating new members into the group, turning them into "made men." In David Cronenberg's *Eastern Promises* (2007), the character played by Viggo Mortensen becomes a made member of the Russian Mafia through a ceremony in which he is asked if he will renounce his father (who was a stool pigeon against the Mob). Mortensen replies "yes" and attempts to say something positive about his mother, only to be cut off by a high-ranking member, who tells him provocatively that his mother was a "whore." Mortensen accepts this subserviently and deferentially, knowing full well that to become a true made man, he will have to reject his past, and his real family, symbolically and literally, by pledging exclusive allegiance to the clan, which has become his only family.

## RITUALS AND RITES

Ritual weaves a feeling of magic on believers and specific groups (and even entire societies), but rituals and attendant rites can, over time, suffer from the erosion of significance. So, to maintain their control over group members and preserve a collective identity of the group, Mafia organizations revise their own rituals in terms of the convenient fictions provided by popular culture (movies and television). This "resemblance effect" is achieved with characters and places in the movies that remind us of real people and familiar settings, as well as plots that focus on issues of common concern (love, happiness, relationships, marriage, children, and so on).

People do not grasp reality directly, but through representations (words, symbols) of it. In a fundamental way, all representations are fictive, because they do not tell the real story of existence, only a selective and interpretative version of it. Criminal organizations certainly have grasped this basic principle of the human mind, manipulating fact with fiction to produce a mystique for themselves.[1] In fact, much of the Mafia allure captured in movies and real life revolves around symbols associated with ritual mysticism (symbols borrowed from religious orders, secret societies, and other groups), mystification (unique bits of language), and styles of self-presentation (a strategic use of images). There is drama associated with Mafia rituals, even if many of its actual ceremonies are quite unglamorous and dull to outsiders. Criminal groups are what the sociologist Emile Durkheim calls "segmentary societies," that is, groups whose survival depends on producing "mechanical solidarity" through a ritualistic replication of existing cultural forms.[2] Ritual is the first phase in achieving replication and thus obtaining consensus to the cause from new recruits.[3] It thus re-creates the identity of the new member, fashioning it in conformity to the expectations of the group. The objective is to impart to the participant a new belief system and role as part of a new family, as well as how he is supposed to relate to others.

The rites used have been shaped liberally from those of both the secret societies of the past, like the Freemasons, and religious and chivalric practices.[4] Alongside the Mafia's money and violence, the folklore surrounding its connections to ancient rites is a powerful tool for instilling fear in outsiders and promoting silent conformity among members. Given the large presence of Freemasons and other secret societies in Sicily—for instance, a Masonic sect named the *carbonari* ("charcoal burners") became a subversive political group who wanted to unite Italy—it is probable that the arcane oaths and ceremonies used by the Mafia today originated in these societies. As John Dickie notes, "More than anything else about the Mafia, the initiation ritual bolsters widespread myths about how ancient the organization is. In reality, it is as modern as everything else about the Mafia. It was almost certainly borrowed originally from the Masons."[5]

The rituals of Masonic secret societies were brought to Sicily from France via Naples around 1820. There they became somewhat fashionable among opponents of the Bourbon regime at the time. Masonic societies took an oath of secrecy and had initiation bloodletting rites and other ceremonies that the Mafia clearly seems to have "cut-and-paste" for its own purposes. The first description of the ritual of allegiance is found in a police report of 1876, in Palermo, regarding a Mafia clan led by Antonio Giammona, one of the first infamous Mafia bosses in the postunification period of Italy. The ritual is described as follows:

> The boss pricks the index finger of the initiate. He then lets the blood from the finger fall onto a sacred image, which is then burned and put in the hands of the initiate, who is expected to hold the burning artifact. The burning image symbolizes the fate that the initiate will suffer if he were ever to betray the clan.[6] (translation ours)

According to scholar Giuseppe Giarrizzo, in eighteenth-century Masonic groups both within and outside of Sicily, a betrayer was called *infame*, a designation later adopted by the Mafia.[7] Giarrizzo further notes that it is from Masonic ideology that the Mafioso concept of humility and total submission derives. The Italian word *umiltà* ("humility") is rendered as *umirtà*, following a dialectal pattern in Sicilian of rendering "l" as "r." And from this the word *omertà* emerges.

Ritual differentiates criminal organizations from common street thugs. It allows them to create bonds, trust, and a shared system of symbols among members. And by connecting them to secret societies of the past, it ensconces the view about themselves as ancient warrior organizations. The following citation of a Mafioso initiate allows us to get a glimpse into this mind-set:

> You must forgive me for this distinction I make between the Mafia and common crime, but it's important to me. It's important to every Mafioso. We are Mafiosi, the others are just the rabble. We are men of honor. And not so much because we have sworn an oath, but because we are the elite of crime. We are very much superior to common criminals. We are the worst of all![8]

If one adds to this sense of superiority the power of organizational structure, it is easy to see why the Mafia continues to be successful. John Lawrence Reynolds puts it as follows:

> Primitive in terms of other, more beneficent institutions such as governments and the Catholic Church, the Mafia nevertheless managed to develop a configuration that exerted discipline and control over its members. Over time, it crafted the group into an effective power in the same manner that disorganized guerrillas are transformed into an effective fighting force by adapting the techniques of a regimented and motivated army.[9]

## RELIGIOUS SYMBOLISM

There are two ways in which religion is exploited by the Mafia. One is by expecting members of the Mob to show devotion to the Church; the other is to adopt and adapt religious symbols and rites for its own purposes. In other words, outward faithfulness to Catholic practices (baptism, confirmation, marriage) is part of the display of omertà meshing with the use of in-group practices and ceremonies that mirror religious practices in form and symbolic content. By invoking the names of saints and adopting sacred forms of ritual, the criminal organization maintains its connection to the broader forms of meaning that constitute the culture in which it exists. It is little wonder that the Italian

Mafias trace their origins to religious events and figures. Members are typically practicing Catholics who show themselves to be devoted to the sacraments and the Church in general. In fact, they often negotiate deals and plan operations during baptisms, marriages, and other religious ceremonies.[10] Religion is thus a cover for the conduct of criminality and establishing allegiance to the group. For the 'Ndrangheta, the *cumpari* ("godfather") is the archetypal figure of the extended family, assigning to him the same religious duties that a real *cumpari* is supposed to accept. Here again, *The Godfather* has had a direct impact on how the criminals now conduct their rituals and perceive themselves. The 'Ndrangheta now considers the relation between *cumpari* and *figlioccio* ("godson") an important one in its model of family structure.[11] This creates powerful loyalty under the guise of religious duty.

Religious marriages, too, allow the criminals to establish blood and family linkages. The marriage ceremony brings the different criminal families together, just like in *The Godfather*, to discuss the meaning of their differences and seek consensus on various issues. The marriage ceremony and feast thus provides a context for intergroup discussion and the negotiation of new partnerships and business transactions.[12] What could be more "honorable" and "respectful" than a contract killing negotiated during a sacred marriage or the performance of some sacramental rite? The twisted irony is ludicrous, yet deadly real.

Quotations from the Bible are found throughout the documents of the criminal syndicates rounded up by the police. The reason for this is obvious. In the same way that televangelists play liberally on the Bible for self-serving purposes, so too do Mafiosi use it to justify their deeds. One criminal organization, the Sacra Corona Unita ("United Sacred Rosary"), which is based in the Puglia region, has even named itself after a powerful religious artifact, the *sacra corona* ("sacred rosary"), which will purportedly "unify" the members (*unita*) as if in a prayer-based group. The following aphorism by French poet Edgar Quinet is clearly applicable to the Sacra Corona Unita: "It is certain that if you would have the whole secret of a people, you must enter into the intimacy of their religion," for this guarantees allegiance to it.[13] Police raids of the homes of Mafiosi and Camorristi have uncovered religious icons and artifacts scattered throughout them. The Mafia is seen as a honorable gang, in part, because of this allegiance to traditional practices and its obvious dislike of the modern world's nihilistic values, which they see as foolish and going against the traditions and history of the true Italy. This displayed worldview, as opportunistic as it is, has great appeal to many in an age of postmodern nihilism, which has left young people, in particular, searching for the kind of values and ethics that Mafiosi espouse in their own feigned fashion. The open display of religiosity is highly attractive to many young people today.

The deliberate connection to religion on the part of Mafiosi is also evident in the fact that many vendettas and murders are planned to coincide with religious feasts or to be carried out at sacred sites and places (cemeteries, sanctuaries, and the like). As mentioned in the first chapter, a famous vendetta slaying occurred on St. Valentine's Day in 1929. Seven members of the George "Bugs" Moran gang were assassinated in a North Clark Street garage of Chicago as part of an internecine gang war for control of the lucrative illicit liquor trade. Police suspected the Al Capone gang of carrying out the execution, but they were never able to prove it. Interestingly, the primary target, Moran, was not among the dead for the simple reason that he had slept in. The fact that it took place on St. Valentine's Day speaks volumes about how the Mafia does such things. It may be coincidental in this case, but it is nonetheless emblematic of how Mafia operations unfold—symbolically and brutally at once.

What does the Church think about all this? The position of the Church on the Mafia has been vague in the past. Being the center of social activities in rural areas, a tacit acceptance of clan members was a practical reality. They belonged to the community and were practicing Catholics, even though everyone knew who they were. In many cases, the Mafiosi were held in high respect by both the community and clerics. A convenient eye was closed. In the last few years, all this has changed, in part because the Church is no longer the center of social life, and in larger part because of the changes in Church philosophy, for instance, ecumenism. In many regions, parishes have joined the anti-Mafia movement that sporadically surfaces in southern Italy. This development traces its origins to 1993, when the late Pope John Paul II turned to Mafiosi while visiting Agrigento in Sicily and implored them publicly to abandon their criminal ways. It is no coincidence that the Pope was not Italian and, thus, did not fully grasp the nuances of the Mafia–Church connection. In 2009, the Church proclaimed that there was no need to excommunicate alleged members of the Mafia, the

'Ndrangheta, and the Camorra because their criminal activities in themselves put them automatically outside the Church. But the Church is ultimately powerless in excluding the Mafiosi from attendance and devotion, no matter how immoral they may be judged to be, because of its theology of forgiveness and all-inclusiveness.

Together with threats and intimidating gestures made toward individual priests by Mafiosi, the Church is, and has always been, powerless in doing something about the Mafia. All a Mafioso has to do to make sure that a knowing priest will keep his silence is to confess the relevant act to him in a confessional. The seal of confession is binding on the priest who hears the confession not to divulge criminal acts. There is also the constant intimation of conspiracy that surrounds the uneasy relation between the Mafia and the Church, as *The Godfather, Part III* insinuates. In the movie, we can see snippets of this suggestion when, for example, Michael Corleone makes a deal with the Vatican's finance minister, whom he is paying for a loss of funds, in exchange for a controlling share in a European mega company.

Some would claim that, because of historical links to the Church, the Mafia is little more than a branch of the Church, but this is incorrect. The Mafia borrows from Church symbolism and creed, but it distorts them to its own requirement of self-justification, in the same way that it distorts the code of chivalry. As Dickie aptly puts it,

> Like Mafia honor, Mafia religion helps Mafiosi justify their actions— to themselves, to each other, and to their families. Mafiosi often like to think that they are killing in the name of something higher than money and power, and the two names they usually come up with are "honor" and "God." Indeed, the religion professed by Mafiosi and their families is like so much else in the moral universe of mafia honor, in that it is difficult to tell where genuine—if misguided— belief ends, and cynical deceit begins. Understanding how the Mafia thinks means understanding that the rules of honor mesh with calculated deceit and heartless savagery in the mind of every member.[14]

It came as little surprise to Mafia historians and critics when Italian police found a list of "Ten Commandments" in the hideout of a Mafia boss in 2007. The comparison of these to the Ten Commandments of the Bible was clearly deliberate. They are commandments for the made man:

1. No one can present himself directly to another of our friends. A third person must do it.
2. Never look at the wives of friends.
3. Never be seen with cops.
4. Do not go to pubs and common clubs.
5. Always being available for Cosa Nostra is a duty, even if your wife is about to give birth.
6. Appointments must be absolutely respected.
7. Wives must be treated with respect.
8. When asked for information, the answer must always be the truth.
9. Money cannot be appropriated, unless it belongs to others or to other families.
10. Anyone who has a close relative in the police, anyone who has a two-timing relative in his family, anyone who behaves badly and immorally, cannot be a member of Cosa Nostra.

The Mafia clearly sees the modern world to be "unnatural" and "immoral." By adopting commandments, the made man can see himself to be above the herd mentality of others and express his superiority freely over them by the use of violence. This justifies their activities by putting them on the side of "the right."

The first commandment is consistent with an ancient chivalric rule of conduct. A man of honor cannot be so brutish as to introduce himself to another man of honor. This must be done through a third member who knows both and will thus introduce one to the other. In this way, the honor of both is guaranteed. As part of the introduction protocol, the presenter utters the following: *"Lui è come noi oppure lui è la stessa cosa"* ("He is like us or is the same thing").[15] This ritual is intended to confirm and strengthen omertà. The individual has no worth without espousing this code. After the first encounter, Mafiosi of the same clan often greet one another with a kiss. It is a sign of recognition and brotherhood.

The third and fourth commandments impel Mafiosi to set themselves apart from outsiders. The third requires no comment—simply put, being seen with cops is a capital sin. The Mafia has its own vigilante means to carry out a vendetta against anyone who has perpetrated some injustice against its members or their families. As the fourth commandment implies, not being seen at social club venues and pubs implies that the Mafioso must stand apart from the riffraff who socialize in indiscriminate ways. The only friends that the Mafioso is allowed to have are other Mafiosi—other men of honor. The second and ninth commandments define relations among the members, paralleling the content of two biblical commandments related to adultery ("Thou shall not covet thy neighbor's wife") and stealing ("Thou shalt not steal"). The difference is, of course, that the real commandments refer to adultery and stealing in general, while these refer to adultery and stealing within the clan. The seventh commandment informs the Mafioso always to treat his wife with respect. The fifth, sixth, and eighth commandments inform a Mafioso how to act and behave with regards to his superiors. A Mafioso must always be on alert and prepared to act on a moment's notice for the Mob.

The tenth commandment incapsulates the essence of what omertà is about. A Mafioso must behave morally, never using foul language or obscene gestures in public. He is a "knight in shining armor." Silence is golden.[16] He also cannot have a "two-timing" relative, implying guilt by bloodline association. Violation of any of these commandments is punished accordingly. For minor offenses, a common form of reprisal is the *sfregio sulla guancia* (cheek cut), which permanently marks the offender as a transgressor. For serious offenses, like going to the police, it is death.[17]

Oftentimes, the vendetta is announced in some symbolic way. In the movie *I cento passi* (2000), directed by Marco Tullio Giordana, sending a tie to a transgressor is a sign of disloyalty, indicating a hangman's noose. It has the following message: "If you do not shape up, you will find yourself hanging from one of these." Needless to say, the commandments never refer to homicide or death directly, since these would raise awareness as to what the Mafia is fundamentally all about—terror, power, and murder.

The Yakuza have developed a strikingly similar set of six principles by which members are expected to live and abide. They are as follows:

1. Never reveal the secrets of the organization.
2. Never violate the wife or children of another member.
3. No personal involvement with narcotics is allowed.
4. Do not withhold money from the gang.

5. Do not fail in obedience to superiors.
6. Do not appeal to the police or the law.

Another principle adopted by the Yakuza is that a member must never use foreign words. Yakuza slang is fanatically chauvinistic and tribal. Even the youngest Yakuza recruits are expected to avoid using trendy American words. It would dishonor the Yakuza code to import into the clan foreign rubbish that relates to the impure secular world of global culture.

The Triads of China have a similar set of oaths, which an initiate is required to recite. There are thirty-six in total. These are inscribed on sheets of paper in the lodge where the initiation ritual takes place. In one of these, the new member swears loyalty to his fellow members and declares that he will never deceive or be disloyal to them. In another, he promises to help the families of other members if asked to do so and always be courteous and friendly toward them. In another oath, he pledges never to betray the secrets of the organization to outsiders. Once a member, there is no turning back, as the oath stipulates: "If I should change my mind and deny my membership of the Triad I will be killed by myriads of swords." One oath in particular encapsulates what outlook on life the new member is supposed to adopt: "I shall be loyal and faithful and shall endeavor to overthrow Ch'ing and restore Ming by coordinating my efforts with those of my sworn brethren. Our common goal is to avenge our Five Ancestors." The Ch'ing and Ming were dynasties in China, and this allusion to the past is intended to connect the Triads to Chinese history.

Criminal societies have created for themselves covert cultures complete with rituals and symbolism. The initiation rites of these groups require the prospective member to undergo a symbolic death and rebirth—"dying" from his previous life to be "reborn" into a new life. By taking oaths, the member knows full well that disobedience will mean reprisal and even death. As in a religious cult, the initiate is expected to follow the commandments until his dying day. He must always obey the leader's orders; ask permission on all important matters; never lie to another member; and, above all else, take an oath of silence.

## INITIATION AND PASSAGE RITES

Perhaps the most crucial of all rituals in criminal organizations are those that bring a new member into the fold. These mark his entry into a new life, helping him understand and accept his new role. A preinitiation trial period is often required. To be eligible for initiation into the Mafia, the prospective member might have to participate in a killing, known as "making bones." The candidate will then wait to be asked to attend a special meeting of the clan that he has decided to join. Clan members sit around a table. After answering the clan's questions, the process of being "made" in the mold of a Mafia knight begins for the candidate. Significantly, the ritual involves holding the burning image of a saint and reciting an oath of secrecy and obedience. The clan leader will then take a knife and cut the candidate's trigger finger. The blood from the finger symbolizes both his own death and that of those that he will eventually have to kill. Death in the case of the candidate is both metaphorical (leaving behind his previous life to be reborn into the new one) and literal (since if he breaches trust he will end up dead). The burning part of the ritual is also symbolic of metaphorical death.

It was Joseph Valachi's testimony before a Senate subcommittee (chapter 1) that uncovered this aspect of Mafia culture. Later, another informant, Tommaso Buscetta, gave more explicit testimony to the Italian authorities. Both emphasized the critical importance of the initiation ritual, since, as Paul Lunde notes, it binds the initiate to the clan for life:

> Initiation consisted of a blood oath and an oath of obedience. The aspiring member had to be presented for initiation by at least three "men of honor" from the family. Blood was drawn from the initiate's finger and sprinkled on the picture of a saint, which was set on fire and passed from hand to hand while the initiate swore to keep the code of Cosa Nostra, which he was bound to for life. His *cosca* was his new family, and he could not switch allegiance.[18]

Most initiation rites involve three stages. First, a participant is temporarily separated from the rest of society and his former roles within it. During the transitional stage of the ceremony, the participant is expected to pledge allegiance to a set of principles and beliefs that he is expected to adopt and enact in his life. After this, he is formally admitted into the clan. Participants in most rites don or utilize special symbols to emphasize their temporary separation from society and represent the changes they are expected to undergo. Incantations and oaths are also often used to bring about emotional responses.

The 'Ndrangheta, for example, uses an invocation ceremony, alongside the use of hand gestures that resemble those in prayer. These are meant to impart to the new recruit a sense of spiritual rebirth in the transition from his previous life to his new one. Called a "baptism," the ceremony involves assigning the epithet of *picciotto* to the neophyte, who invokes Santa Liberata and the Archangel Gabriel. The recruit pledges his undivided loyalty to his new family, sealing it with a prayer. The ceremony is called *taglio della coda* ("cutting the tail") because the *picciotto* is viewed as entering the clan as an animal with a tail, an appendage that only serves to stir up dust as he walks. After the cutting of the tail, he will no longer make dirt, since he will from then onward walk on a *tappeto di erbe e fiori* ("a carpet of grasses and flowers").[19] This liberates him symbolically from his previous state of ignorance, introducing him into one of *furbizia* ("wise-guy-ness"). The former state was devoid of *sangue e onore* ("blood and honor"), which is precisely what the participant is supposed to seek in his transition from his previous life to the new one.

The choice of Santa Liberata is hardly arbitrary. She is a widely venerated saint who is often depicted with two children in her arms and considered to be the patron saint and protector of children. She is the protector of the new child, the *picciotto*, who has been born again into the new church of the *Onorata Società*. The born-again feeling that this imparts is immeasurable, since it is not rational, but emotional. As George Bernard Shaw once put it, "The great danger of conversion in all ages has been that when the religion of the high mind is offered to the lower mind, the lower mind, feeling its fascination without understanding it, and being incapable of rising to it, drags it down to its level by degrading it."[20] Invoking the Archangel Gabriel as a witness to the rebirth is also emotionally strategic, since in the New Testament it is he who announces to Mary that she is to be the mother of Jesus (Luke 1:26–1:31). Significantly, the Annunciation is also summoned during a subsequent passage rite to the higher echelon of *camorrista* in the clan hierarchy. The *picciotto*'s index finger—the trigger finger—is pricked so that a few drops of blood will fall on an image of Mary. A candle is lit to burn the image so that it can be destroyed by fire, as the *picciotto's* protector and supporter during the previous apprenticeship period speaks the following words, warning him that if he does not keep the code of honor he will be similarly destroyed:

> *Come il fuoco brucia questa immagine sacra così brucerete voi se vi macchierete di infamità. Se prima vi conoscevo come un picciotto da ora in poi vi conosco come un camorrista.* ("As the fire burns this holy image so too will you be burned if you become sullied with infamy. If before I knew you as a *picciotto* from now on I will know you as a *camorrista*.")

Fire represents purification and the attainment of wisdom. It makes the *picciotto* worthy of being called an 'Ndranghetista. It also implies taking risks, for the initiate is expected, symbolically and literally, to show his courage and allegiance by putting up with fire burning in his hand. He cannot show any signs of suffering, which would show him to be unmanly and thus unworthy of belonging. Blood has always been a symbol of rebirth in Mafia rites. It also represents sacrifice, being part of a consecrated offering made to the other clan members to establish and perpetuate a sacred bond between them.

During the passage rite to the role of *sgarrista* in the 'Ndrangheta, an image of the head of Saint Michael the Archangel is shredded as it is being burned. Then, a cross is carved out on the participant's right thumb with a knife. This symbolizes the fact that Michael was the leader of the angels (Daniel 10:13, 10:21, 12:1) and guardian angel of Israel. He is also considered to be the immediate lawgiver to Moses on Mount Sinai (Acts 7:38). The *sgarrista* is expected to be a leader of other clan members. Moreover, like Michael, who slew a dragon (Revelation 12:7–12:9), he is expected to become a fearless warrior. The leader of the clan consecrates the member to the new role by uttering an oath that makes reference to three knights who cut off Michael's head:

> *A nome dei tre cavalieri Minofrio, Mismizzu e Misgarro che hanno tagliato la testa a San Michele Arcangelo, perché è stato molto severo nella sua spartizione, e il suo corpo è stato sepolto sotto due pugnali incrociati e la sua testa è stata bruciata. Con la sua cenere di battezzo e ti consacro sgarrista.* ("In the name of the three knights Minofrio,

Mismizzu, and Misgarro who cut off the head of Saint Michael the Archangel, because he was so severe in his partition, and his body was buried under two crossed daggers and his head burned. With his baptismal ashes I consecrate you to the order of *sgarrista*.")

The three unknown knights represent demonic forces that must be overcome by a *sgarrista*. Significantly, the name *Michael* signifies "he who is like God," and that is exactly what a high-ranking 'Ndranghetista is supposed to aspire to be. A half-burned image of the Archangel Michael—the kind used in initiation rites of the 'Ndrangheta—was found in the wallet of one of the victims massacred in a Calabrian family feud carried out in Duisburg, Germany, on August 15, 2007.

The use of such rituals, however, raises the question of conscience and how the mobsters reconcile religion with criminality. The reconciliation can, perhaps, be explained with cognitive dissonance theory. The term was coined by the American psychologist Leon Festinger, who defined it as the strategy of explaining a condition of conflict or anxiety resulting from an inconsistency between one's beliefs and one's actions.[21] People will seek out information that confirms their own attitudes and views of the world or reinforces aspects of conditioned behavior, avoiding information that is likely to be in conflict with their worldview, since this will bring about cognitive dissonance (a sense of anxiety).

Festinger initially conceived of the theory after reading an item in a newspaper that bore the headline "Prophecy from Planet Clarion Call to City: Flee That Flood," in reference to a UFO doomsday cult that had been told by the leader that the end of the world would come to pass on a certain date. The prediction, however, did not come about. The disconfirmed expectancy caused dissonance in all group members. Some abandoned the group when the prophecy failed, but most attempted to downplay the event by accepting a new belief, namely, that the planet was spared because of the group's resolve and faith. Festinger claimed that when people become uneasy and anxious after facing information that conflicts with their belief systems, they develop strategies to attenuate the dissonance they feel and often turn the contrasting information on its head, so as to make sense of it in terms of their belief system. One cannot simply join the Mafia or the 'Ndrangheta off the streets. He must wait to be admitted by showing his mettle and evaluated as a potential "knight of the order." This might involve killing someone. This act binds the member to the clan for life, since the alternative (viewing the act as one of brutal murder) would create dissonance. The murder is thus justified as part of an honor code.

The aforementioned rituals do indeed allow criminals to resolve cognitive dissonance since they evoke religious feelings and thus a higher cause. This is also why at each successive point of passage to the higher echelons of the clan, the religious symbolism becomes ever more binding. For example, in the 'Ndrangheta, the use of keys alludes to the biblical story when Jesus gave Saint Peter two keys—one gold and one silver—the former opening the kingdom of heaven and the latter symbolizing the spiritual authority of the pope on earth.

A transcript of a recording made by the New Jersey police on July 19, 1990, in a house in the Bronx of five initiates into Cosa Nostra, brings out all the implicit premises, concepts, oaths, and beliefs connected with the initiation rite itself. We provide relevant excerpts here from that transcript (AP = Anthony Piccolo, acting boss; PM = Pasquale Martirano, prominent member of the Philadelphia crime family; GF = George Fresolone, an initiate):

> AP: If you stay you become part of us, then you have to do the right thing. Here it's no bullshit, plain English. This is a family, you stay with the family, I'm your family. We can help each other. It's got to be with the family. No outsiders. Anybody approaches you, it's another place, it's another family, you report to your man, whoever's in charge. Don't let nobody try to bullshit you, say hey this and that. This is our family, and that's the way it stays.
>
> PM: You're supposed to live by the gun and die by the gun, live by the knife and die by the knife.
>
> AP: This is a thing of honor. This is not a thing of business. A lot of people misunderstand that. This is honor. You've got to be a honorable person. . . . You don't talk about none of your friends, because we become brothers. You don't talk behind them, you got something to say, you see who's in charge, get it squared away, and that's the end of it.
>
> [Beginning of ritual of puncturing the finger and burning a sacred image]
>
> PM: Here know what you do? Come on George [an initiate]. I need a match. Or a cigarette lighter. . . . Give me your hand George. Got no blood George.
>
> GF: (laughs) That's alright.

[As the initiates hold the burning image in their hands each one speaks]

"May I burn in hell if I betray my friends in the family."[22]

Initiation rites are found also in many motorcycle gangs. To join the Hells Angels, a prospective member must undergo an apprenticeship or trial period. The member must also know quite a lot about motorcycles and take part in "runs" as part of his apprenticeship. Once the member is accepted, he must assume a series of servile tasks to show his loyalty, including cleaning the clubhouse and washing motorcycles. After this period, the member is given his color, designating his rank. He can now vote at meetings. Like a Mafioso, a "member is required always," writes Lunde, "to place the group before his family and business interests," and those "who breach the rules can expect severe punishment and expulsion from the organization."[23]

The policeman W. P. Morgan gave the world a glimpse into Triad initiation rites in 1960, by publishing an account of his interviews and experiences with the gang. The rite takes place in a lodge, which represents the mythical "City of Willows," and is headed by an Incense Master dressed in white alongside the group's leader, dressed in red. All other members present are dressed in black. Color plays a significant role in marking rank and importance. The rite starts with a dance, as the prospective member approaches from the east gate, where he is challenged by another member, with whom he is expected to exchange a ritual handshake. Next he passes under swords held in the form of an arch and through three more gates guarded by statues of famous Triads. He then reaches the altar, stepping through a bamboo hoop. This has historical significance. It alludes to the legend of monks escaping from the Shao Lin monastery, and it symbolizes the member's rebirth into his new family. He then takes the thirty-six oaths (as previously mentioned). His finger is pricked and dipped into a bowl containing spices, wine, ashes, and the blood of a rooster. The concoction is then shared by everyone in attendance.[24] It is important, again, to note how common blood symbolism is in criminal organizations. Some street gangs even name themselves after it, as do the Bloods, a gang originating in Los Angeles whose gang color is that of blood. As the "life fluid," it defines what family groupings are all about, literally and figuratively.

Rites (explicit or implicit) govern virtually every aspect of clan life. To commemorate the death of another Mafioso, the women are expected to dress in black and display their grief at the funeral by crying and praying out loud over the casket, as part of their family duties. As the weeping takes place, the capo, or some other high-ranking member, goes to the mother or wife of the dead Mafioso and attempts to hug her to console her. She is, however, expected to rebuff his consolation, beating her breast with her fists. The Mafioso must nonetheless insist on providing consolation, whereby she finally gives in and allows him to hug her until she stops sobbing to show resignation to the death. By so doing, the woman shows acceptance of the role of the Mafia in her life and acknowledges her submission to its principles of omertà. Such rituals are embedded throughout Mafia culture. As Lunde explains, "The true Mafioso looks after his crime family like a father, often serving as godfather to the children of his underlings, attending their weddings and funerals, and holding frequent, almost ritual banquets, where the seating arrangement reflects each person's status in the family."[25] The son of a Montreal Mafia boss, murdered in 2009, was buried in a gold casket, the ultimate in funerary ostentation. Significantly, a common tradition in the Mafia is that the person who ordered a murder will send flowers to the victim at his funeral, which is also seen in a part of the original *Scarface* movie of 1932, when John Lovo, after ordering the murder of Big Lou Costillo, asks Tony Camonte to send a wreath of white carnations in the form of a cross to the Costillo family.

The Mafia has adopted its own model of the patriarchal family, adapting it to define its own raison d'être. In so doing, it shows its rejection of the larger society's nihilistic deconstruction of the family. The subtext is obvious: The Mafia, like Catholicism, respects traditional values and morals based on the family. This is perhaps what makes the Mafia so attractive to *Godfather*- and *Soprano*-crazy popular culture, which sees the Mafia as an oasis of traditional values in a morass of an "anything goes" culture.

But Mafia culture twists these values for its own criminal objectives. The biblical commandment "Honor thy father" is warped to read "Honor thy capo." The Mafia is all about power—power over women, power over other men, power over the government, and, subconsciously, power over death, since the Mafioso believes that he alone will decide when and how he will die. But such power is achieved, as Sir Walter Raleigh once put it, by devious means and thus has no real import on social development outside the clan: "All, or the greatest part of men that have aspired to riches or power, have attained thereunto either by force or fraud, and what they have by craft or cruelty gained, to cover the foulness of their fact, they call purchase, as a name more honest."[26] And as the American writer James Baldwin so eloquently phrases it, the "relationship of morality and power is a very subtle one. Because ultimately power without morality is no longer power."[27]

## THE POWER OF SYMBOLS

Rituals without symbols would be meaningless. From the beginning of time, people have created symbols to help them understand the world. The Greeks symbolized the sun as the god Helios driving a flaming chariot across the sky, and the Egyptians represented the sun as a boat. In Babylonian myth, the hero Gilgamesh searched for a magical herb that made all who ate it immortal. Symbols stand for the phenomena of everyday life and transform them into abstract diagrams of these events, bearing great meaning. They assign a memorable form to events in the world, requiring no theory or explanatory science to grasp their meaning. They speak their own form of visual language.

The symbols used by the Mafia tap into this "symbolic instinct." As we have seen, the symbols of blood, fire, and hands are common ones. Blood is connected to life and rebirth and to family lineage ("related by blood," "blood is thicker than water," "bad blood"). Blood is also a pivotal part of the Catholic Mass, which is centered on the transformation of the body and blood of Christ into wine and bread. And blood binds people together. Many Asian organized crime organizations allow members through the requirement of *guanxi*, which loosely translates as "blood connections," implying that they must be related by blood or marriage.

The symbolism of blood ties in Mafia culture is explained cogently by Lunde as follows:

> In a world where power was arbitrary, safety lay in the family. The larger and more extended the kinship group, the more protected the individual, especially in a social system of vendettas, where honor demanded that no offense should be allowed to pass unavenged. An

army of brothers and cousins was the best protection in an unjust
world. Nothing is as important to a Sicilian as the ties of blood.[28]

Symbolism affects people emotionally. Take, for instance, the symbolism of stabbing the hand (mentioned earlier). Murder cannot be carried
out without hands; hands are indicative of collaboration (*una mano lava
l'altra*, "one hand washes the other"); and, of course, the hand is a
source of fear if it holds something hidden or dark (*La Mano Nera*, "the
Black Hand").[29] These meanings are all imprinted in the stabbing symbolism.

The "Black Hand" symbol, discussed several times in preceding
chapters, is particularly interesting. There is some controversy among
historians regarding its origin. Some say that the early twentieth-
century gangsters borrowed it from a Serbian secret subversive society
following the assassination of Archduke Franz Ferdinand, heir to the
throne of Austria-Hungary. His murder blocked the possibility that his
sympathy for the Slavs would ease tensions between Austrians and
Hungarians and the Balkans. He had organized a tour of Bosnia-
Herzegovina with his wife, Sophie. As they made their way through
Sarajevo on June 28, 1914, an assassin jumped onto their automobile,
firing two shots and killing Franz and Sophie almost instantly. The
murderer, Gavrilo Princip, was linked to a Serbian terrorist group
called the Black Hand. Gangsters in the United States in the first
decades of the twentieth century were, purportedly, inspired by this
episode.

But, as Cawthorne and Cawthorne observe, this is not a viable theory, because the Black Hand in the United States had been in operation
before the assassination in Sarajevo. In that era, journalist Lindsay Denison attributes the use of the symbol to an older secret society. Writing
in the September 1908 issue of *Everybody's Magazine*, he states that
Black Handers traced their roots to a "secret society [that] fought the
government and the church in Spain during the Inquisition and the [era
of] secret societies of Southern Italy."[30] The president of the United
Italian Societies of New York during the era, Gaetano D'Amato, believed in a similar source for the symbol. He claimed that it had been
used in Spain in the 1860s by a group of bandits who proclaimed themselves to be protectors of the downtrodden and that the term migrated
to the United States "probably by some Italian desperado who had

heard of the exploits of the Spanish society and considered the combination of words to be high-sounding and terror-inspiring."[31]

Whatever its origins, it is clear that the *Mano Nera* symbol, as D'Amato correctly remarks, shows how symbols can be used to instill terror in people. And as Denison goes on to say, it was also effective because the "very names of the Black Hand's big chiefs are names of terror."[32] It was not a Sicilian symbol, however, because "in Sicily," writes Dickie, "this kind of abuse of a criminal logo used by the honored society would have been unthinkable."[33] Black Hand criminal syndicates operated in such major U.S. cities as New York, Philadelphia, New Orleans, San Francisco, Detroit, and Chicago.[34] The idea of a *Mano Nera* coming out of the dark to crush anyone who did not comply with its demands inspired fear and guaranteed compliance to the extortion schemes. A Black Hand letter of threat would also contain some accompanying terror symbol, for example, a noose or gun, and it was signed in frightening black ink. It is reported that the great Italian American tenor Enrico Caruso received a Black Hand letter on which a black hand and a dagger appeared demanding $2,000. Caruso reported the threat to the police, dropping off the money at a prearranged location. Two Italian American businessmen showed up to retrieve the money and were arrested on the spot.

Why would so many people be intimidated by such a symbol? In large part, it was a matter of the lack of trust in the American authorities, which Italian immigrants saw as taking a naïve stance with respect to the criminal gangs, as Cawthorne and Cawthorne point out, stating the following:

> Italian immigrants felt that American law had no understanding of their situation and no power to help them. They knew that the threats in Black Hand letters were likely to be carried out if they did not pay up. Italians were armed. According to an official at Ellis Island, the clearing station for immigrants, two-thirds of all male immigrants landing were carrying knives, revolvers, or blackjacks.[35]

A group of Italians calling itself *Mano Bianca* ("The White Hand Society") was eventually formed, claiming that they understood the character of the gangsters better than the U.S. authorities. The White Handers declared war on the Black Handers in vigilante style, but they did not succeed. The reason was simple: Italians did not believe that they would be any more effective than the authorities in stemming the power of the Black Handers. The code of secrecy that was brought along from the old world reared its ugly head in the new social environment. In Chicago, there was a famous incident involving the notorious "Shotgun Man" in the 1910s, who murdered more than a dozen people in the same area of town, the corner of Oak and Milton (known as "Death Corner"), in broad daylight during ten years of terror. The murderer was never identified, despite witnesses. The code of secrecy allowed the killer to go free. Black Hand practices disappeared toward the end of the 1920s, after public outcries to put a stop to them. The mobsters, however, were resilient, using more subtle methods to carry out extortion.

The Black Hand symbol may be older than many think. Lunde traces it back to Corleone in Sicily:

> A notorious Black Hander was probably the first Mafioso to establish himself in New York. Antonio Morello headed a large family from Corleone, in Sicily. The town remains the base of the most powerful Mafia family on the island and was made famous in Francis Ford Coppola's 1972 film *The Godfather*. Morello is said to have killed up to 40 people in the 1890s. Members of his family continued to operate until the 1930s, and some of his descendants are said to be involved in U.S. organized crime to this day.[36]

Such symbolism is effective because it allows communication to take place by suggestion or innuendo rather than directly, thus creating a "menacing atmosphere" that allows for threats to be made more successfully than if the threats were blatant. The symbols of criminal gangs reach deep into our mythical past. As Reynolds puts it, "Much of the glamour and intrigue that outsiders associate with Cosa Nostra flows from omertà, the code of honor sealed in a secret induction ceremony that presses the sanctity of the code upon is members."[37] It is no coincidence that the symbol of the 'Ndrangheta is the biblical tree of knowledge and that it is the rosary for the Sacra Corona Unita, a breakaway faction founded in Trani Prison in 1981 by Giuseppe Rogoli to resist the attempt of another crime group to move into the region of Puglia. The rosary symbolism taps into a deeply fervent belief system in the Virgin Mary, which is characteristic of Italian Catholicism in general, but particularly of its practice in Southern Italy.

Crime fiction writers are also aware of the power of symbols, starting with the writings of Edgar Allan Poe and Sir Arthur, Conan Doyle. In fact, detective fiction coincides with the rise of forensic science, as Ronald R. Thomas has perceptively written.[38] Today, there is a growing sense among the police and criminologists that to understand crime groups, one must look at symbolism much more seriously. For example, the Center for Homicide Research in New Orleans has adopted specific techniques to investigate crime scenes and decode the symbolism used by criminals and gangs. The courts are also beginning to use semiotic evidence in criminal proceedings. In the city of Edmonton, Canada, for example, the court may look at whether an accused person uses a name, word, symbol, or other form that identifies, or is associated with, a criminal organization to determine whether the accused participates in the criminal organization. As Diego Gambetta argues, the "myth lends force to a reality [that] would not otherwise be able to manifest itself."[39] Demystifying the Mafia means unpacking the artificial meanings of their symbols and exposing their true brutal purpose.

# 4

# APPEARANCE

Every man is the builder of a temple, called his body, to the god he worships, after a style purely his own, nor can he get off by hammering marble instead. We are all sculptors and painters, and our material is our own flesh and blood and bones.

—Henry David Thoreau (1817–1862)

**A**s they say, appearances can be deceiving. In the case of Mafia culture, this is absolutely true. "Made men," as the movies have certainly realized, are attractive because they literally put on appearances, from gangster chic to facial expressions meant to scare people to death. In *The Godfather*, Marlon Brando plays Don Vito Corleone, the capo who runs the Mafia universe from his chair. His body language, stern yet benevolent facial expression, suave clothing, and uncompromising composure in the face of adversity bespeak of an "appearance code of omertà" that, thanks to Hollywood, has become a model even for the real Mafia. Corleone is what a wise guy is imagined to be in both Mafia and popular culture. He is an icon. Like a veritable patriarch, he inspires fear, yet reassurance, by his appearance and his actions. He is even seen playing with his grandson in the movie.

The Mafioso is a chivalrous knight, a character who by force of his impeccable appearance and behavior must exude an inherent inner strength that allows him to keep up a constant "menacing atmosphere" around him. This must always be clear and unambiguous. It is imprinted in his style of clothing, his posture, his walk, and all other aspects of appearance that the made man must convey to others. Any sign of weakness is not tolerated. But are Mafiosi really like this? Photos of Mafiosi at the turn of the twentieth century hardly convey this macho image of the cool, well-dressed gangster. A lot of the actual appearance features associated with the Mafioso persona today actually come from the movies. The reality of Mafia culture today lies in the blurring of lines between fiction and reality. As filmmaker Jean Cocteau once put it, "A film is a petrified fountain of thought."[1]

Mafiosi, like everyone else, model themselves after actors in film. The persona of the Mafioso that comes from the movies and is transferred to real life is a very attractive one, since it taps into the myth of the handsome and fearless "bad boy," who is sexually attractive and exciting at the same time that he is dangerous. This myth is especially appealing to dispossessed youths and those growing up in a Mafioso family. The Mafioso is an "appearance junkie."

The sociologist Erving Goffman points out that everyday life is theatrical, involving a skillful staging of character according to social context.[2] The Mafiosi on the screen and on the streets are indeed "character actors" who adopt a nonverbal code of dress, gesture, posturing, and facial expression to impress one another and identify themselves to others as men of honor. The ancient Greek word *persona* meant, in fact, a mask worn by an actor onstage. The Greeks probably adapted it from the ancient Etruscan word *phersu*. Subsequently, it came to have the meaning of "the character of the mask-wearer" on the stage.[3] Eventually, the word came to have its present meaning of "human being," jumping from the stage to real life, but it still reverberates with theatrical meaning. The linkage between character and the theater has not been missed by modern-day criminals. Their whole business is, in many ways, a performance—a performance of stylish, honorable terror. And it works, because at an unconscious level, we are all affected by the performance.

## THE MADE MAN

As anthropologist Ray L. Birdwhistell observed in his study of body language, nonverbal signals constitute a powerful system of communication because "all movements of the body have meaning. None are accidental."[4] This certainly applies to the Mafia. A capo, being older and wiser, is expected to show a laid-back imperious persona, whereas a *picciotto* would have to put on a different appearance, showing strength of will and, at the same time, an eagerness to please the capo.

Hollywood has been both a documenter and fabricator of Mafioso body language. The ruthless gangster on the screen is a macho figure, complete with mustache, slicked hair, erect body posture, and a gait-style walk. No one can tell him how to behave. And he is a promiscuous man, as emphasized by the movie *Goodfellas* (1990): "Sunday was wives night at the club, but Saturday was girlfriend night." In reality, a large part of the allure of Mafia culture is sex. John Lawrence Reynolds puts it as follows:

> The allure of a secret society, the macho posturing of its leaders, and the immense wealth at the fingertips of its most successful members attracted women to the Cosa Nostra men almost from the beginning. Of course, the reverse was true as well: Many ambitious young Italian men wanted to join because Cosa Nostra members had no trouble attracting good-looking women.[5]

The adoption of a cinema style and look became ludicrously obvious when Cosimo Di Lauro, the son of a notorious Camorra boss, intentionally donned a gangster appearance before the cameras as he left his house handcuffed in 2005. He slicked back his hair with gel and pulled up the jacket collar of his black raincoat in imitation of characters in such cult movies as *The Crow* and *The Matrix*. Hairstyle surfaces every once in a while in Mafia culture as significant. In a famous trial in Calabria in 1890, the members of the *piciotteria* (a forerunner of the current 'Ndrangheta group) were distinguished by the fact that they wore their hair cut in a "butterfly style," with a tuft of hair in the middle that was slicked and combed high toward the back of the head. In 1911, Joe Musolino, a Calabrian gang leader in the city of Toronto who controlled the waterfront, was arrested wearing the same hairstyle, showing that the symbolism of the hairstyle knew no borders.[6]

In the comedy *Analyze This* (1999), a Mafia capo, played by Robert De Niro, begins seeing a psychiatrist, played by Billy Crystal, for therapy, because he is experiencing problems while having sex with his mistress. The reason is that he is having qualms of conscience. The irony is tangible. The true virile *uomo d'onore* ("man of honor") would never be expected to behave or think in this way. One of the members of De Niro's crime family discovers the therapy sessions and proclaims that they are a sign of weakness. The movie is, clearly, a satirical deconstruction of the Mafia persona and a parody of Mafia culture in general. A true Mafioso would never be a part of a culture that espouses psychiatry as a remedy to sexual problems. Real men solve their own problems or take advice from family members, not from therapists. In fact, there are real cases of Mafiosi suffering mental problems who consult psychiatrists in jail regarding a series of personal issues, from losing one's hair to unflattering skin blemishes, showing how paranoid gangsters are, just like De Niro, about appearance and sexuality.

Mafiosi have actually feigned mental illness to save their skins or avoid being jailed. One of the most well-known cases of this is that of Vincent "the Chin" Gigante, who was the Genovese family boss until 2005 and was dubbed the "Odd Father" by the media because he often showed himself in public wearing pajamas, slippers, or a bathrobe, walking along Sullivan Street in Greenwich Village. His appearance was a put-on, a ploy to indicate that he had mental problems and thus that he should not be jailed for his criminal activities, but the police caught on and he was eventually put in prison, where he later died.

Made men must always display their virility. Motorcycle gang members wear leather suits complete with boots, street thugs in Los Angeles wear baggy pants and caps to instill fear in passersby, and so on and so forth. Dress codes might appear ludicrous and even comical to some, but to insiders and those victimized by gangs, they evoke trepidation and even terror. A Mafioso dressed in a black shirt with white tie, donning a mustache and slicked-down hair could easily be seen as a caricature of the gangster—a gangster imitating a gangster image—unless he is coming at someone with a violent intent. The same applies, in a different way, to the modern-day Yakuza, who, instead of wearing traditional Japanese clothing, seem to favor, as Reynolds notes, "tight-fitting silk suits, pointed-toe shoes, slicked long hair in a pompadour style, and a swagger more reminiscent of the sitcom television character The Fonz than of butchers like Vito Genovese and Lepke Buchalter."[7] The appearance cliché is bolstered by the fact that Yakuza members love to drive large and ostentatious American cars, like Cadillacs and Lincolns, rather than smaller Japanese automobiles. Gangster appearance codes are, indeed, part of a construction of a criminal persona that is intended to give the gangster a recognizable look, like a dark knight, and elicit fear in anyone who comes upon him on the streets.

The gangster borrows extensively from popular culture. As part of the code, the typical modern-day gangster has adopted sun glasses, cigars, and a ring for his pinky finger. Dark sun glasses have always stood for toughness and sexuality, as the movies have constantly shown, starting with a famous 1944 photo of movie actor John Ford donning a pilot uniform, with a cigar and dark glasses. The look caught everyone's attention. *Gun Crazy* (1949) was likely the first movie in which a gangster wore sunglasses to convey coolness and toughness at once. Soon afterward, the glasses were adopted by gangsters everywhere as part of the evolving new appearance code. In Sicily, Prince Alessandro Vanni Calvello Mantegna di San Vincenzo, suspected of having Mafia connections, was invited to a reception in honor of Queen Elizabeth II during her visit to Palermo in 1982. A photo taken at the reception showed the prince standing to the left of the Queen wearing sunglasses, which stood out incongruously.[8]

## TATTOOS

In the initiation ceremony scene in *Eastern Promises*, Viggo Mortensen sits in his underwear in front of a panel of members of the Russian Mafia who are reading the tattoos on his body in an effort to literally "read his character." The tattoos reveal that Mortensen was a thief who had spent time in a Siberian prison and that he was noncooperative in prison, spending a lot of time in solitary confinement. After Mortensen passes the initiation test, he is marked with three new tattoos, including a ten-pointed star on each shoulder near the collarbone and a star on his knee. These indicate his status as a new member of the Russian Mafia. At that point, a higher-ranking member looks at the knee star and says to it, "So he won't get down on his knees before authority." Tattoos are part of the appearance code in many criminal gangs. They constitute a visual language identifying the gang to which a member belongs, recording his personal biography or his autobiography, along with describing his strengths, accomplishments, and opinions. They constitute a pictography of the criminal mind.

Tattooing is one of the most ancient forms of body decoration. Some anthropologists date it to around 8,000 BCE, but it may go back even farther in time.[9] Almost every culture has practiced tattooing at one time or another. As early as 2,000 BCE, the Egyptians used it to indicate social rank and affiliation. The ancient Greeks and Romans, on the other hand, used tattoos to brand slaves and criminals. In the Marquesas Islands, a group of islands in the South Pacific Ocean, they are revered signs of honor. In eastern New Guinea, tattoos on young women are signs of beauty. The list of cross-cultural functions of tattooing could go on endlessly.

The importance placed on the role of tattoos in character portraiture by the Russian Mafia was first brought to wide attention by the documentary film *Mark of Cain* (2000), which consists of interviews and conversations in a Russian prison. The aforementioned line spoken by a high-ranking member in *Eastern Promises* was taken word-for-word from the interview of an inmate in the documentary. Tattoos have specific meanings. For example, getting a tattoo of the image of famous communists like Lenin, Stalin, and Engels on one's chest meant a death sentence; however, the inmate would not be shot because that would imply shooting the famous image. Knuckle tattoos identify a prisoner as a convicted armed robber, while the tattoo of a ring on a prisoner's finger represents a journey through a juvenile correctional facility. Tattoos of churches stand for beliefs. As one prisoner puts it, "Each cupola is a conviction." As mentioned earlier, the star tattoo on a knee means that the gangster will not get down on his knees before authority, as another prisoner pointed out. Those who wear tattoos as fashion statement or to brag about themselves will have them cut off, "along with his skin," declares another prison interviewee. A tattoo in criminal culture is not a fashion statement; it is a biographical statement. As one prisoner states in the film, "You don't have the right to tattoo just anything."

The cult of prison tattooing can be traced back to the 1920s, when tattoos were used by prisoners to recount their criminal activities, as well as to show contempt for the authorities. Many of these early criminal tattoos remain as part of prison symbolism to this day. Their meanings are self-explanatory:

*Skull on a finger*: Means that the wearer is a murderer.
*Barbed wire across the forehead*: Represents a life sentence.
*A spider's web*: Indicates that the wearer is a drug addict.

*Head of a tomcat*: Stands as a good luck sign.

*SS runes*: Denotes that the wearer is not a stool pigeon (informant).

A *dagger running through the neck from shoulder to shoulder*: Implies that the wearer is a sex offender and that the tattoo was applied forcibly on the wearer.

*The pointed star on each shoulder* (in Russian prison culture): Indicates the length of the prison sentence, one point for each year. [10]

Prison tattoos vary from country to country. In Ireland and Britain, the acronym ACAB tattooed between the knuckle and first joint may mean either "Always Carry A Bible" or "All Cops Are Bastards." This tattoo is sometimes shown as a series of dots, similar to the Morse Code. Tattoos can also be involuntarily administered as a type of punishment or shame for betraying some code of manliness or honor.

Extensive body tattoos (known as "body suits") are commonly worn by Yakuza members. These are called *irezumi* in Japanese. The size, shape, configuration, and color of the tattoos denote not only the wearers' affiliation, but also his ability to withstand pain. Initially, tattoos were signs of nobility and social distinctiveness in Japan, and they were often used to indicate status. The use of tattoos by criminals started in the Kofun period (300–600 CE), when they were placed on criminals by authorities for identification purposes, much like the brand marks put on cattle. At the start of the Meiji period (1868–1912 CE), the authorities banned tattoos worn in public because of their criminal connotations, so tattooing continued underground. It was legalized after the occupation forces entered Japan in 1945. Many businesses in Japan still ban customers with tattoos. As Antonio Nicaso and Lee Lamothe point out, the original Yakuza criminal tattoo was a band "inked around a criminal's arm, with each ring indicating a crime committed"; it was, in effect, a "permanent marking that displayed the adherent's permanent self-expulsion from society." [11] Throughout time, entire bodies have been covered in tattoos, in large part to allow new members to show their endurance for pain and thus their commitment to the organization.

Tattoos constitute the hallmark of membership for many gangs. Wearing unearned tattoos is seen as a punishable offense in the criminal world, with discipline ranging from the painful removal of the tattoo to death. The tattoo must be earned by some action that is deemed to be valiant in criminal terms. Bragging rights come only through actions.

Not all criminal organizations, however, endorse the use of tattoos. Many would consider them to be a breach of omertà. The modern Mafia does, however, tolerate individual tattooing, recognizing it as a trend and nothing more.

## GANGSTER CHIC

In 2011, newspapers across Italy reported that the new governor of Ucciardone prison in Palermo had attempted to put a stop to the practice of prisoners wearing designer clothes and flashy jewelry. Unlike many countries, prisoners in Italy are not required to wear standard uniforms. The power of dress among made men was not missed by the governor. The nickname of that prison was "The Grand Hotel," because of its lax conditions with regard to uniforms, turning it into a Mafia fashion show. One Mafia capo is reported to have celebrated his birthday with champagne and lobster, dressed in fashionable evening attire. This has prompted comparisons with the film *Goodfellas*, in which Robert De Niro and Joe Pesci lived the high life behind bars. Images of Mafiosi wearing designer silk clothes in prison are something that the governor was clearly attempting to stamp out.

Clothes constitute a special kind of nonverbal language. Because they are worn on bodies, they are perceived as extensions of physical appearance. As British fashion designer Katharine Hamnett once remarked, "The origins of clothing are not practical. They are mystical and erotic. The primitive man in the wolf-pelt was not keeping dry; he was saying, 'Look what I killed. Aren't I the best?'"[12]

As part of his character, the made man must aspire to be attractive and virile. As Paul Lunde puts it, the made man must always put on an appearance that is dignified so that he can "accumulate that precious commodity respect," allowing him to "create authority" and power.[13] But the gangster chic that is evident today in criminal lifestyle was not always the rule. "Early Mafia dons," write Nicaso and Lamothe, "often resembled peasants in appearance, wearing homespun clothes and living in modest houses."[14] The early Mafiosi put on a public face of modesty, not gaudy ostentatious fashion. Indeed, in the era of Prohibition, the gangsters were among the best dressed patrons of the nightclubs, establishing a gangster chic that common people tried to imitate.

Historically, the first period of gangster fashion consciousness in southern Italy was documented at the turn of the twentieth century, when extradited criminals from the United States came back all dressed up in style. They wore white shirts, elegant suits, and, most importantly, donned fedora hats, rather than the *coppola*, a traditional flat cap worn by men in southern Italy. Hats were signs of class distinction at the time, and the *coppola* represented peasant status, while a hat, like the fedora, was a sign of high class status. Ironically, the returning immigrants were typically paunchy or potbellied, unlike their Italian counterparts, which was also interpreted as a sign of well-being and wealth. Initially, the Italian bosses rejected this new style, considering it to be useless and simply showing off, pointing out that, "*I colori attirano le mosche*" (literally "colors attract flies," meaning the police). One of the most renowned bosses, Giuseppe Genco Russo, who ruled in the period after World War II, would wear only a cotton white shirt, dark pants, and a shabby hat to emphasize the need for real Mafiosi to dress down and be inconspicuous. Another boss, Paolino Bontade, who was well-connected politically, also wore a simple gabardine suit that was made by a local tailor. It was in the 1970s that things started turning around, when gangsters in Italy finally started catching the "sartorial bug" and becoming as fashion conscious as their American counterparts. In fact, Bontade's son, Stefano, was nicknamed "The Prince" because of his demeanor and sober elegance. The real leader in fashion, however, was Tommaso Buscetta, who became an icon of gangster chic with his blue blazer and fashionable gray pants. Dolce & Gabbana was so impressed by his wardrobe that it adopted his style to launch a clothing line, after Buscetta turned informant.

That gangster chic was reflected in the criminal characters of such movies as *Little Caesar* and *Scarface*. It consisted of a neat, stylish look—suit, tie, and hat—that was not, however, pretentious or affected. Al Capone's wardrobe was the perfect model of the appearance code. In the 1920s, he built a criminal empire in Chicago that is still imitated as a model for organized-crime operations. Capone was known as "Scarface" because he had once been slashed on his left cheek in a fight that had left three scars. The scars became a symbol of the "cut face," the sign for a vendetta. He was the picture of gangster chic, always dressed in a suit, tie, and hat. His hair was slicked down and his manner of speaking subdued, yet authoritative. Capone was a celebrity, and he lived like one, often seen riding in an armored limousine to theaters and sports venues, where he entertained guests in private boxes. He was convicted of income tax evasion in 1931. After eight years in prison, he retired to his mansion near Miami, where he died on January 25, 1947, from complications due to syphilis. His appearance belied his brutality. Although it was never proven, there is little doubt that he was responsible for the St. Valentine's Day massacre, captured many times on film, including Roger Corman's *St. Valentine's Day Massacre* (1967) and Billy Wilder's 1959 comedy *Some Like It Hot*. The FBI agent who hounded Capone was Eliot Ness, who has been immortalized by the television series *The Untouchables* (1959–1962) and Brian De Palma's film *The Untouchables* (1987).

A close rival to Capone, both in criminality and fashion, was Lucky Luciano, who also appeared in public in a suit and tie and wore his thick hair in a slicked-down fashion. Luciano cofounded the New York syndicate in the early 1930s, an organization that still guides the structural changes and operations of Cosa Nostra. His suave appearance blended American and Italian fashion styles. He fashioned a "new look Mafia" in every sense, including the adoption of a distinctive weapon, the "tommy gun," a type of submachine gun named after its inventor, army officer John T. Thompson. The gun was actually introduced into Mafia culture by George "Bugs" Moran, another fashion-conscious gangster of the early era. Like in the cowboy movies, where wearing a distinctive holster and gun was de rigueur, so too for Cosa Nostra, the tommy gun became part of the appearance code. Lunde explains the role of the tommy gun as follows:

> Although it could deliver bullets at a rapid rate of fire, the gun was only really effective at close range. It was the ideal weapon for urban warfare, if you didn't mind killing bystanders. George Moran's gang was the first to use it, but gangsters everywhere soon took it up, paying as much as $2,000 per weapon. The Thompson submachine gun was the classic gangsters' weapon. [15]

Elegant suits and a tommy gun became the classic gangster look in the era of Prohibition. Another legendary mobster, Frank Costello, stretched this look to its limits. As Reynolds notes, "Costello was the original dapper don, sporting thousand-dollar tailored suits, custom-made shoes, perfect manicures, and a bullet-proof haircut." [16] Facing tax evasion charges, Costello was advised by his lawyer not to dress pretentiously in court because it would turn off the mainly middle-class jury members. The lawyer said, "Start wearing cheap suits, old shoes, a lousy tie. You'll do better with the jury." Costello replied, "I'd rather lose the goddamn case."[17] Costello became a fashion icon and celebrity writ large. He was imitated by many other gangsters and was probably the model for Don Vito Corleone, played by Marlon Brando, in *The Godfather*. Costello had a raspy voice, and there is little doubt that Brando adapted it for his role.

Styles have, of course, changed, but images of men in suits carrying tommy guns are indelibly imprinted in the popular imagination, thanks to the movies. Mafia men today wear designer clothes, as the governor of Ucciardone prison found out. Heroes must look good, no matter who they are (be it criminals or lawmen). The uniform is now part of omertà. Today, criminals are arrested as they eat caviar and drink champagne, like the 'Ndrangheta boss Pasquale Condello, or dressed in a moncler jacket and T-shirt, like Giovanni Nicchi, a flamboyant and young Mafia boss; however, there are some Mafiosi, like Bernardo Provenzano, who are throwbacks to a previous era, intentionally wearing peasant clothes and living in rustic abodes. In fact, Provenzano was arrested as he was eating ricotta cheese and a plate of chicory, the utmost symbol of humble living.

Today, the most elegant Mafioso is also the most feared and most wanted by the authorities. His name is Matteo Messina Denaro, also known as "Diabolik," known for wearing Armani and Versace clothing and who also has the reputation of a Don Juan. His nickname derives from the fact that he adored the character of Diabolik of comic-book fame, wanting to adopt the symbol of the machine gun on the hood of Diabolik's car. Denaro has fashioned himself as a real-life comic book character. He is known to have once said to a friend, "I can build a cemetery for all those I have killed." Another boss known as much for his brutality as for his foppishness was the late John Gotti, known as "Dapper Don," who also loved to put on a show in front of the cameras.

## ENTER THE MOVIES

The way Mafiosi dress and look is mirrored in movie portrayals, which, in turn, influence how Mafiosi will look and act. This dynamic extends to symbolism, like the so-called Mafia kiss. Real Mafiosi will kiss each other to indicate loyalty and mutual respect. Some kisses, however, are more famous than others, because they have been captured on film. One of these is the kiss between the Mafioso Totò Riina and former prime minister Giulio Andreotti. Andreotti's last term coincided with the so-called *mani pulite* ("clean hands") trials, targeting corrupt politicians. In 1995, Andreotti himself was put on trial in Palermo for involvement with the Mafia. The *pentito* Balduccio Di Maggio testified that Andreotti had exchanged the Mafia's kiss of respect with Totò Riina, who was a fugitive at the time. Whether this was true is a moot point. Without the media, that purported kiss would have never become a symbolic act connected to the level of corruption that had beset Italian society.

Kissing to show respect is found across Mediterranean societies. In Mafia culture, the kiss may mean something quite different. Called the "kiss of death," it was revealed to the world by a movie, *The Valachi Papers* (1972), based on Joseph Valachi's testimony in 1963. The kissed person is marked for death, alluding unconsciously to the biblical story of Judas. Valachi had testified before Arkansas senator John L. McClellan's Permanent Subcommittee on Investigations of the U.S. Senate Committee on Government Operations. During his testimony, he came forward with the story of a capo giving him a kiss on the cheek, which he interpreted as a "kiss of death." That event is referenced in *The Godfather, Part II*, when Michael Corleone kisses Fredo, who had turned informant, as he utters, "I know it was you Fredo, you broke my heart."

Without the movies, such gestures would have remained largely unidentified. The movies have become both documenters and manufacturers of Mafia lifestyle and codes since at least the early 1930s. Take, for example, the movie *Donnie Brasco* (1997), which is loosely based on the real-life events connected with Joseph D. Pistone, an FBI agent who successfully infiltrated the Bonanno crime family in New York City during the 1970s, under the alias "Donnie Brasco." The character of Donnie Brasco is played by Johnny Depp, who met with Pistone several times while preparing for his role. After it was revealed that Donnie Brasco was an FBI agent, Dominick "Sonny Black" Napolitano was murdered for having allowed the agent to infiltrate the family. He was shot dead, and his hands were cut off. It was not another informant who gave him away; it was the movies.

The link between the Mafia and the movies is something that the Mafiosi themselves have exploited. When Lucky Luciano returned to his hometown of Lercara Friddi in Sicily, he financed a movie theater there. The first film projected was the Italian version of *Little Caesar*. Luciano often recounted that people would come to him on the streets and kiss his hand in recognition of his generosity and because, as he boasted, they wanted to show him that he was more worthy of adulation than Little Caesar.[18] The *Valachi Papers*, adapted from Peter Maas's book of the same title, tells the story of Joseph Valachi, the first American Mafia informant. The movie was instrumental in telling the story of the real Mafia to society at large. For instance, in the movie, there is a reference to the use of concealed weapons in a violin case, which is an intrinsic part of Mafia lore, part fact, part fiction. We also see Mafiosi spying on one another, showing pictures of other families to killers so that they can become familiar with their targets—all behaviors that are similarly part of the same lore. The importance of choosing the appropriate weapon is seen in an episode where a gun and a knife are placed on a table in front of Joseph Valachi, played by Charles Bronson. He is told menacingly by the capo that anyone who lives by the knife and the gun will die by the knife and the gun—a version of the biblical warning, "For all they that take the sword shall perish with the sword" (Matthew 25:52). It is no coincidence that this very text is found at the beginning of the 1931 movie *Little Caesar*. The capo then recites three rules to Valachi—rules used in a "time of war," referencing the ten commandments of the omertà code (discussed in the previous chapter). The merciless use of the vendetta is seen in another episode, where the penis of a man who slept with the capo's mistress is cut off.

Mafia portrayals in the movies have not only influenced the perception of criminals, but also, by extension, Italian Americans in general.[19] The disclaimer at the beginning of the *Godfather* and *Scarface* movies about claims to authenticity actually "demonstrates," writes Cortes, "a recognition that entertainment films do, in fact, teach, possessing the power to create, reinforce, and modify public images about ethnic

groups, including Italian Americans."[20] Early silent era films represented the desire of Italians to melt into the American cultural pot. Significantly, as Cortes continues, they "seldom participated in such silent film
social deviance; their days of widespread screen gangsterism would not
arrive until the 1930s."[21] The subtext in the early movies was that by
abandoning the previous ways through hard and honest work, the immigrant could easily climb the American social ladder. Things changed
radically in the 1930s, when, along with Chinese Americans (*Chinatown
Nights*, 1930; *The Mysterious Mr. Wong*, 1935) and Irish Americans
(*Public Enemy*, 1931; *The Roaring Twenties*, 1939), Italian Americans
turned into gangsters in the American imagination (*Little Caesar*, 1931;
*Scarface*, 1932). This was further entrenched in such postwar movies as
*Black Hand* (1950), *The Brothers Rico* (1957), *Inside the Mafia* (1959),
and *Pay or Die* (1960). Cortes concludes the following:

> Such movies not only reinforced the gangster image of the *Little
> Caesar/Scarface* tradition, but also added a new dimension. Larger,
> better organized, and far more brutal than their film predecessors,
> these Italian American movie gangs also enjoyed venal connections
> with international Italian criminality, a far cry from the bumbling
> Italian soldiers of World War II Hollywood lore.[22]

Many critics see *The Godfather* movies as an exception to this pattern of
portrayal, since they purportedly delve into other aspects of Italian
American culture, for example, its fervent insistence on moral values
and ethics and the family as the central institution of society, but we beg
to differ. The problem in these movies is that the values are embodied
by mobsters and their families, not common Italian Americans. It is no
wonder that Italian American groups assailed *The Godfather* as creating
a false image of all Italians. Aware of the problem, Italian American film
directors started deflecting the spotlight away from Mafia culture to
other gangsters, implying that gangsterism is not exclusive to Italians,
but part of human life. Brian De Palma's 1983 remake of *Scarface*
includes Cuban Americans in the gangster mix. Predictably, there was
an outcry from the Cuban American community, which, like similar
protests by Italian American groups, was short-lived and ineffectual. A
*Godfather*-style disclaimer is found at the end of the movie. It reads,
"The characters do not represent the Cuban American community, and
it would be erroneous and unfair to suggest that they do," which indi-

rectly emphasizes this very representation. That is, by actually alerting audiences to the Cuban American community, their tendency is to read the movie as a nonfiction narrative.

Not to be outdone, Michael Cimino turned his lens on New York's Chinatown criminal gangs with the *Year of the Dragon* (1985). As had the Italian American and Cuban American communities, Chinese Americans protested, but again to no avail. Like *Scarface*, *Year of the Dragon* proclaimed that it was about a "group of ruthless criminals" who should not be seen as being typical of any specific ethnic group. Even Italian director Sergio Leone joined the fray with his 1984 movie *Once Upon a Time in America*, portraying the rise of Jewish American gangs in New York during the first years of the twentieth century with Ennio Morricone's haunting score.

Significantly, *The Godfather* captures the fancy of real-life gangsters, who responded enthusiastically to the film. Salvatore "Sammy the Bull" Gravano, the former underboss in the Gambino crime family, stated, "I left the movie stunned. I mean I floated out of the theatre. Maybe it was fiction, but for me, then, that was our life. It was incredible. I remember talking to a multitude of guys, made guys, who felt exactly the same way."[23] The portrayal of Don Vito Corleone was scriptwriter Mario Puzo's idea of what a Mafioso was supposed to look like and how he was expected to act. His hunch paid off handsomely and, more importantly, had a ricochet effect on Mafia culture itself. But the verisimilitude was not totally made-up, as Lunde points out, writing the following:

> Although it is sometime claimed that the Corleone character was modeled on Carlo Gambino, he is, in fact, much closer to the traditional Sicilian "godfathers" like Don Calogero Vizzini or Joe Masseria than he is to more recent dons like Carlo Gambino. Puzo summed up his feelings about latter-day dons when he said, "A guy like John Gotti wouldn't last a day in Sicily."[24]

The choice of the name *Corleone* was also no accident. It is the name of a town of 14,000 inhabitants just south of Palermo. In his novel *Il gattopardo* ("The Leopard"), Giuseppe Tomasi di Lampedusa describes it as a harsh place with downtrodden people constantly facing travails. In that environment, it is little wonder that Corleone was the birthplace of one of the earliest Mafia strongholds. Likely derived from the name of an Arab fighter, *Kurliyun* ("Lionheart"), the town has a long tradition of exhibiting public courage and standing up to injustice. In the second half of the 1800s, Corleone became the center of the farmer uprisings against the large agricultural estate holders. The town also boasts of a warrior, sword-wielding patron saint, Saint Bernard, who, as a poor cobbler in the seventeenth century, defended the indigent and women against corrupt aristocrats before donning the hood of the Capuchin monks. It is "no coincidence," writes John Follain, "that the townspeople called Don Michele Navarra, the founding father of the Corleonese clan [that] was to overwhelm the mafia like no other in its history, *'u patri nostru* ("Our father")—just the way they referred to God."[25] It is also not a coincidence that Don Vito Corleone had many of the same characteristics of Don Michele Navarra: "Like a deity the doctor [Navarra], a short, corpulent figure with a bull-like neck and a broad, apparently kindly face, had the power of both life and death over every single one of them."[26]

The public loved the movie. The closely knit Corleone family stood out to audiences as a model of the traditional family. The movie struck a resounding chord in the American psyche. Only a Don Corleone could make things right in America, if he were given a chance. Even top Mafioso Joe Bonanno was quoted as saying, "This work of fiction is not really about organized crime or about gangsterism. The true theme has to do with family pride and personal honor. That's what made *The Godfather* so popular."[27] During his 1986 trial, Luciano Leggio took a page from the movie. Dressed elegantly in a dark suit, striped tie, and pocket handkerchief, he had with him a giant, thick cigar, which he would take out from time to time from his inside pocket, playing with it in a twirling motion, in obvious imitation of Don Vito Corleone, sniffing it continuously without ever smoking it. The theatrical performance was transparent. As Follain writes, Leggio was playing to the cameras: "The cigars were only props in Leggio's imitation of Marlon Brando's Don Vito Corleone in the film *The Godfather* and were for the benefit of the television cameras."[28] John Dickie describes Leggio's performance and appearance in the following way:

> And with his cigar, his long, heavy jaw, and his arrogant bearing, he actually managed to pull it off; there is more than passing resemblance between the two. In fact, Leggio's face was already infamous before *The Godfather* was released. The anti-Mafia commission's

analysis of Leggio, published in the same year that the movie came out, is not a document that tends to dwell on anything as frivolous as appearances. Yet, it was transfixed by Leggio's "big, round, cold face," his "ironic and scornful" glower. If the cinematic Don Vito was the face of the Mafia as it likes to think of itself—judicious and family-centered—then Luciano Leggio's features, by contrast, were an emblem of capricious terror. Whereas Brando's heavy lids gave his character an almost noble reserve, Leggio's staring eyeballs suggested that he was as volatile as he was malevolent.[29]

The use of cigars by gangsters actually goes back in time and can be seen in movies like *Scarface*, based on the life of Al Capone, who would rarely be caught without a cigar in front of the cameras. Significantly, Carmine Galante, a New York Mafia boss, was gunned down while having lunch at a restaurant in Bushwick, Brooklyn. The police found him with a cigar stuck in his mouth. Galante's nickname was "Cigar," and it is likely that the killers either kept it there symbolically or inserted into his mouth to make a brutal statement.

Interestingly, the influence of the movie extended beyond the United States. It is reported that Triad enforcers, who have always couched their threats in symbolic ways before taking retributive action, used an episode from *The Godfather* to formulate a threat against a Hong Kong businessman. As Reynolds writes, he "was sent the severed head of a dog" by the enforcers, who were obviously "impressed with the celebrated scene, incorporating the severed head of a horse from *The Godfather*."[30] A similar event occurred in Sicily in 1991, when a horse's head, with a knife stuck in it, was found in the car of a construction company that had refused to pay the *pizzo*. Indeed, many Mafiosi, like Antonino Calderone (a state witness), not only saw the movie or read the book, but became indelibly influenced by it. Calderone tells of a homicide ordered by Mafia boss Totò Di Cristina after having read the book, where he tells his hit men to dress up as doctors (as in the book) to go to a hospital and murder a rival.[31]

The movie starts with someone looking for "justice" to be carried out, because the law had failed to do its job. So, the person asks Don Vito for help, while attending his daughter's wedding. Don Vito asks, "Why did you go to the cops, why not come to me first?" This opening scene sets the tone for the entire movie, which revolves around the role of omertà in Mafia culture, even though shady deals and vendettas occur behind the façade of honor. The Mafia's form of justice is direct, in classic Western cowboy style; civil justice, on the other hand, is beseeched by legal entanglements and portrayed as effete, not to mention corrupt. Don Corleone expresses this sentiment, saying, "A lawyer with his briefcase can steal more than a hundred men with guns." America's secret admiration of this form of carnal justice was a part of what made the movie a blockbuster. In the mind of many, things are made right with fists and the gun, not with endless reams of legal red tape. In a way, the movie was a treatise in what is wrong with the American system of justice, at the same time that it showed how vendetta justice cannot, in the end, really solve anything, no matter how glorified it is. As French philosopher Simone Weil so aptly phrases it, "There is one, and only one, thing in modern society more hideous than crime—namely, repressive justice."[32]

The images that came out of *The Godfather* have remained imprinted in everyone's mind. Its residues can be seen in such media descendants as *The Sopranos*, which began airing on HBO in 1999, and subsequent crime movies. People living in the United States and other parts of the world have learned about the Mafia through movies and television. As Reynolds observes, it is through exposure "to *The Godfather* movies or an episode of *The Sopranos*" that most of us now know that the "Italian organized gangs are as rigidly structured and tightly controlled as any corporation."[33]

The movies create reality by simulating it. The world on the screen is a fantasyland that feeds our need for escape from the triviality of everyday life. By seeing the Mafia and other criminal organizations as vehicles of this escape, they gain in significance, making it harder to combat the organizations politically and legally. The movies bring their own reality into the world. Consider the emergence of motorcycle gangs. While gangs have always existed in the United States, as elsewhere, motorcycle gangs surfaced in considerable numbers only in the mid-1950s. It is no coincidence that this occurred simultaneously with the popularity of *The Wild One*, a 1953 movie starring a young Marlon Brando as an outlaw biker. The image of the biker as a sexually attractive outlaw, fearing no one, caught America's fancy, leading to the growth of bike gangs shortly thereafter. The motorcycle replaced the cowboy's horse, offering escape from ordinariness and dullness—a lure that many young people were incapable of resisting. The first motorcycle gang was the Hells Angels, which was founded only a few years earlier than the Brando movie, on Independence Day 1947, in Fontana, a steel town close to Los Angeles, when, to quote Lunde, "4,000 bikers rode into town on a spree that left 500 injured and, following the call-out of the Highway Patrol, 100 bikers in prison."[34] From this, a spirit of friendship was born among the imprisoned bikers. Others also supported their "cause" to ride the bikes freely on the highways of America. The term *Hells Angels*, an appropriate metaphor, was first adopted by the San Bernardino chapter of the club in 1948. The name may have been taken from the prewar film written with an apostrophe, *Hell's Angels* (1930), directed by Howard Hughes, or it may be an invention. The gang borrowed the deathbed insignia worn by World War II fighters for their emblem. Significantly, the Hells Angels came to broad public attention only after the Brando movie.

There is also little doubt in our mind that popular conceptualizations of the Russian Mafia also come from the movies. The existence of a Russian Mafia came to general public awareness after *The Mark of Cain* and *Eastern Promises*, which, as previously discussed, brought to the screen tattooing and initiation practices of the gang. As Lunde points out, the Russian Mafia grew up in prisons during the Soviet era, when a criminal code was created to give the prisoners a sense of organization: "Those who followed the code had to swear, among other things, never to work legitimately; to support other criminals; and to have nothing to do with the state."[35] They came to be called "thieves in law," suggesting that they were bound together by the code. The visibility of the group remained obscure, however, until the movies stepped in to put the spotlight on it. "The term *Mafiya*," writes Lunde, "was first used by the Soviet defense attorney Konstantin Simis in the 1970s," having obviously been under the spell of Hollywood Mafia iconography.[36] He was referring not to the prison gang, but to the bribes and corruption present in the Communist Party.

It was in the late 1980s, at the end of the Soviet era, that the ranks of the Russian Mafia started proliferating. In that decade, the first movies dealing with "other Mafias" started hitting the screen, and, by the time of *Eastern Promises*, they were part of pop culture's expanding world of criminal celebrities. In a similar fashion, the movie *The Yakuza* (1974) brought awareness of the Japanese organization to American popular culture, rebounding back to Japan, where it enabled the real Yakuza to grow even more in size and prestige. The image of a brutal but honorable bunch of modern-day criminal samurai was bolstered by subsequent movies, including *Black Rain* (1989). The Triads made it to the silver screen through the movies of the first legendary martial arts hero, Bruce Lee. Films like *Enter the Dragon* (1973) featured Triad fighters, enhancing the appeal of both the martial arts and the criminal lifestyle of these "noble warriors" in the west, where recreational karate classes grew immensely in popularity in the 1970s because of the movies.

It should not come as a surprise that the movies not only helped construct the image of the made man, but that the Mafia also became involved in the movie business. During the Capone era, the movie business was the fourth-largest industry in the United States. Many of the crime movies in the early 1930s were shot in Chicago, and the Chicago Mafia saw its opportunity to get a cut of the movie pie by taking over movie trade unions, while running extortion rackets on movie theater chains. "By controlling the unions," Lunde observes, "they could cripple any studio that refused to pay protection against strikes," and they could "close down all the theaters in the country with a single telephone call."[37] This came to an end in 1943, however, when three Mafiosi, Johnny Roselli, Frank Nitti, and Paul Ricca, were indicted for extortion. At their trial, the involvement of the Mafia in Hollywood came out, and the Mafia's dream to control movies came to an end.

We agree with Lunde that the rise of the gangster movie in the era was the result of social conditions. He explains the following:

> The popularity of the gangster films of the 1930s is understandable. The movies were made when the Depression was at its worst, and depicted the hopelessness of the time, the sense that the American Dream had ended, and that the world was, in reality, a cold, lonely place where the only law that counted was the gun.[38]

But beyond social conditions, the appeal of the gangster movie has, in our view, deeper psychological roots, tapping into a sense of fear and awe for the outlaw figure and the secrecy of criminal lifestyles. As French author Georges Bataille so fittingly puts it, "Crime is a fact of the human species, a fact of that species alone, but it is above all the secret aspect, impenetrable and hidden. Crime hides, and by far the most terrifying things are those [that] elude us."[39] In effect, the boundary line between fiction and truth, theater and reality, is often blurred because we seek the messages that are found in fiction.[40]

Mafia culture has always understood the power of fiction. They took advantage of the popularity of Pietro Mascagni's *Cavalleria rusticana* to imprint an image of themselves as bandit knights indelibly into Sicilian and, later, Italian culture. The Mafia wanted to "systematically confuse Sicilians and the Mafia," as Dickie remarks.[41] That mistaken association persists to this day, in part because of the movies and, in larger part, because it is convenient for the Mafia to forge the link even more so. As Dickie goes on to comment, "Sicilian culture was for too long confused with *mafiosità* ('mafia-ness'), and that confusion served the interests of organized crime."[42] It was only after the testimonies of the first informants that the veil of secrecy surrounding the Mafia was removed. In a world of total silence, the Mafia thrived. In the spotlight of real cameras, it had to adapt. And it did, taking convenient tips from such movies as *Little Caesar* and *The Godfather*. The myth of rustic chivalry was deconstructed with trials revealing how vile and heinous the gangs were. We mention here the valiant crusade of Italian magistrate Giovanni Falcone, who eventually died at the hands of the Mafia, along with his wife and three bodyguards, on his way into Palermo on May 23, 1992, but his fearless legacy continues to influence everyone who believes in real, not trumped-up, models of chivalry, inspiring anti-Mafia movements in Sicily and elsewhere. By demystifying the forms of fiction behind the Mafia and other criminal groups, we will be able to go a long way toward defeating them. Dickie aptly concludes the following:

> If Cosa Nostra exists, then it has a history, and if it has a history then, as Falcone often said, it had a beginning and it will have an end. Because of the work of Falcone, Borsellino, and their colleagues, as well as the collapse of the cluster of untruths surrounding the notion of "rustic chivalry," historians can now research the history of the Mafia with more confidence and insight than has ever been the case.[43]

What is truly surprising is that despite the movies and the trials that have put the Mafia into a global spotlight, the Mafia has changed very little. It is a secret society that continues to seek power and gain through the art of murder.

# 5

# NAMES

In real life, unlike in Shakespeare, the sweetness of the rose depends upon the name it bears. Things are not only what they are. They are, in very important respects, what they seem to be.

—Hubert H. Humphrey (1911–1978)

**N**icknames are memorable and more likely to stand out than real names because they are more colorful and vivid. For criminals, they are part of how they define themselves, alluding to something in a gangster's character, appearance, or background that is thought to have import or significance. Lucky Luciano, born Salvatore Lucania, was called "Lucky" because of the noticeable large scars around his neck that permanently recorded his fortuitous escape from death after being slashed and left dead by criminal rivals. The nickname of "Scarface" was given to Al Capone because, as previously mentioned, he was involved in a fight that left him with three noticeable scars on his face. These became a personal brand, emphasizing his toughness and fierceness. In fact, Mafiosi have been long aware of the brand value of names. Frank Costello, known as the "Prime Minister" of Cosa Nostra in the 1930s and 1940s in the United States, was quoted by *Time* magazine as stating, "I'm like Coca-Cola. There are lots of drinks as good as Coca-Cola. Pepsi-Cola is a good drink. But Pepsi-Cola never got the advertising Coca-Cola got. I'm not Pepsi-Cola. I'm Coca-Cola because I got so much advertising."[1]

As we saw in the previous chapter, Luciano Leggio was a ruthless gangster who put on a good show for the cameras. The nickname of *La primula rossa* ("Scarlet Pimpernel"), by which he was known, probably comes from the 1935 movie of that name, a remake of an early silent version that revolves around an aristocratic hero during the French Revolution who hides his identity as an idle, useless person but masquerades as the mysterious hero Scarlet Pimpernel, who gallantly rescues aristocrats sentenced to death. Leggio was certainly gallant in appearance but vicious in his life. He was also nicknamed "The Professor," probably because of his inclinations to pontificate to other clan members. He had other names as well, as John Follain elucidates in the following:

> With a round, flabby face, full lips, and a scornful stare, Leggio was referred to—only when safely out of hearing—as "the Grain of Fire" because of his short temper or "the Cripple" due to a slight limp. He suffered from Pott's disease, a tuberculosis of the spine [that] gave him back pain, fever, and heavy sweats at night.[2]

A gangster is a nobody until he is given a nickname. As Antonio Nicaso and Lee Lemothe aptly observe, all thieves have nicknames, as part of the remaking of their identity. Made men are renamed men.

> Those who are brought into the formal underworld may have had nicknames in their former lives; however, when initiated they're given new names or allowed to choose one. Some names describe a physical characteristic—Vyacheslav Ivankov, for example, was called "Yaponchik" because of the Asiatic cast to his eyes. Others might be for a thief's attitude: "Tank" or "Dashing." A home invader might be called "Madhouse" because of his single-minded wrecking of a victim's house.[3]

Interestingly, the head of the *Casalesi* clan (in a province of Caserta), Francesco Schiavone, was dubbed "Sandokan," because his dark beard resembled that of a popular star in a 1970 television series. In the minds of gangsters, there can be many "Francesco Schiavones," but there can only be one Sandokan. This is because nicknames promote distinctiveness. As American writer Florence King aptly puts it, "In its purest sense, nicknaming is an elitist ritual practiced by those who cherish hierarchy."[4] But the use of verbal ritual does not stop there. Criminal organizations also require a brand name for themselves. From "Mafia" to "Hells Angels," these identify the group and its overall character, as well as often telling an implicit story about the group's origins.

## THE GANG

As discussed earlier, the origin of the word *Mafia* is not certain, although some historians trace it to either *mahyas* ("exaggerated boasting"), *marfud* ("rejected"), or *ma fi* ("It doesn't exist"), all Arabic words.[5] Others trace it instead to two other possible Arabic sources—*mahfaz* ("protection") or *mahfil* ("a gathering"). All make sense, given the origins of the Mafia as part of *cosca* culture, and because of Middle East settlements and the linguistic influence of their languages in Sicily. Sicily was colonized from the eighth century BCE by Greeks, who displaced the earlier Phoenician settlers. The island was then conquered by Carthaginians, who, in turn, were conquered by Romans in the third century BCE. Sicily came under Norman rule in the eleventh century, forming the nucleus of the Kingdom of the Two Sicilies, consisting of Sicily and southern Italy. Thus there were many linguistic sources from which the term *Mafia* could have arisen.

Some see its origin as an acronym (also as previously discussed). One possibility is *Morte Alla Francia, Italia Anela* ("Death to France, Italy Cries"), which purportedly came into being during the Sicilian Vespers in 1282. Closer in time to the present, another possibility is "*Mazzini Autorizza Furti Incendi*" ("Mazzini Authorizes Robberies, Arson, Poisoning"). This is an obvious attempt to link the Mafia with the nineteenth-century nationalist movement spearheaded by Giuseppe Mazzini. These origin scenarios are now largely discarded, even though they continue to have adherents among Mafiosi, since it seems to imbue the name with historical relevance. As Lunde puts it, "Most definitions seek to give the Mafia an ancient origin."[6]

As discussed in chapter 1, the term *Mafia* came into general use after an 1863 play by Giuseppe Rizzotto and Gaetano Mosca entitled *I mafiusi di la Vicaria* ("The Mafiosi of the Vicaria"). The word caught on because it referred to secret criminal gangs, being a kind of general term that appeared in 1868 in Traina's bilingual *Italian-Sicilian Dictionary*, where it is defined as "the actions, deeds, and words of someone who tries to act like a wise guy."[7] A later dictionary, published in 1878, claims that the word had been imported into Sicily by Piedmontese bureaucrats and soldiers after Italian Unification, which is an unlikely theory. A scholar of Sicilian culture, Giuseppe Pitré, denied the existence of a Mafia crime gang, claiming that the word simply meant self-respect and personal justice. Actually, the adjectival form of the word *mafiusu* was in vogue in Sicily for centuries to describe a coquettish young girl, called a *mafiusiedda* or a *picciotta bedda* ("a beautiful little one"). But as Nicaso and Lemothe point out, this is really wishful thinking. The fact remains that the term has always defined a criminal gang no matter what its true origins:

> These definitions were well-received by Sicilian society, giving self-justification to any number of antisocial or criminal acts. In truth, these traits, even absent of criminal activity, are nonetheless antisocial concepts that refuse to bow before the laws of either church or state. That such men could come into conflict with the law—particularly if they're engaged in criminal activities—makes a strong underpinning for a cohesive mafia-like mind-set.[8]

At the time of Rizzotto and Mosca's play, the Sicilians knew that street criminals existed, but that's what they were—street gangs. Assigning the name *Mafia* to the thugs gave them an identity and a sense of importance. The term became a one-word history book, allowing for confabulated notions to take root that have become almost impossible to eradicate. Without the play, it is unlikely that prisoners—which the play is about—would be identified in any unique way. In the play, the prison gang had a capo, an initiation rite, and a code of omertà, and it dealt in extortion activities. From this world of fantasy, the Mafia emerged as a social force. The Mafia of the play, and of real life, finds its strength in that code and in the institution of the family. Blood does not betray, and, if it does, the punishment is exacted in blood, as Nicaso and Lemothe write:

> Whatever the true roots of the Sicilian Mafia are, and whatever origin of the name, the organization is the most cohesive and active of all the criminal groups in the world, with the possible exception of Chinese Triads. The Sicilian Mafia has endured oppression by governments and armies, survived incredibly bloody internecine

warfare, and sullied the accusations of informants. In times of power and prosperity, the Sicilian Mafia has extended its reach around the world, at times influencing, if not controlling, international drug trafficking. And after periodic government crackdowns, the Sicilian Mafia has always been able to quietly regroup and bide its time. It has never disappeared.[9]

An interesting take on the origin of the word *Mafia* comes from the pen of novelist Leonardo Sciascia in his 1973 story *Philology*, which takes the form of an imaginary conversation between two Sicilians about the meaning of the word. The older of the speakers, who appears to be a politician, traces it to an Arabic source; the younger of the two prefers to explain its origins as a slang term for manly swagger. As it turns out, both men are Mafiosi, and their dialogue is a rehearsal in case they are called on to testify. Their intent is to confuse. As John Dickie points out, Sciascia is suggesting that "the name 'Mafia' became the Sicilian Mafia's own little joke at the state's expense."[10]

Traditionally, the Sicilian Mafia was based in the western part of the island of Sicily, around Palermo and Trapani. After World War II, it expanded its base of operations to the eastern part. Today, it is active throughout Sicily and Italy. And, of course, as Cosa Nostra, it had already become part of American culture by the end of the nineteenth century. Today it is a global empire with its tentacles reaching everywhere, involved in both criminal and legitimate operations. And, arguably, this is all because the name caught everybody's fancy and stuck.

As also detailed in chapter 1, the first recorded incident of Mafia crime can be traced back to 1890 in New Orleans, when a group of Sicilian Mafiosi killed a chief of police who had been harassing them with arrests. The criminals were acquitted because the witnesses were apparently bribed or threatened. A lynch mob dragged the Mafiosi into the street upon their release and shot or hanged eleven of them. The Mafia seemed to be dead in America, but it was reborn as Cosa Nostra because of two events. One was Prohibition, starting in 1919, which created, as John Lawrence Reynolds puts it, "a low-cost, high-demand, and high-profit opportunity for criminals, especially those operating within an organization that could manufacture, import, and distribute its products under the noses (or with the collaboration) of law enforcement."[11] It is highly ironic that a Puritan-based strategy for stopping the consumption of an "evil liquid" was the pivotal event that allowed Cosa Nostra to take root in the United States.

The second event was Benito Mussolini's crackdown on Mafiosi in Sicily, which led to many emigrating to the United States, joining the emerging Cosa Nostra clans involved in bootlegging. After Prohibition, a solid organizational structure within Cosa Nostra was in place that allowed it to branch out and spread its reach throughout the United States and Canada. Timing was fortuitous for the criminals. Cosa Nostra used the same symbols, rituals, and organizational structure of both the Sicilian Mafia and the 'Ndrangheta, reflecting a hybrid form of criminal culture, waving such requirements as blood ties for membership and expanding its recruitment procedures beyond the Italian heritage pool. Cosa Nostra welcomed Irish, Jewish, and other gangsters into the fold, reflecting, in its own way, the melting pot philosophy of the country to which it had migrated. In a phrase, Cosa Nostra has always been an equal opportunity employer.

As Dickie elucidates, the origins of the term in no way meant a restructuring of the code of omertà or the structure of the Mafia:

> It was in the years following the Second World War that the Sicilian Mafia probably began to refer to itself as Cosa Nostra—"our thing." It may be that the most recent of the Mafia's many names is an American import. The theory has been put forward that the term originated in Sicilian immigrant communities in the United States; it was "our thing" because it was not open to criminals from other ethnic groups. But because the Mafia does not leave written minutes of its dense, cryptic internal conversation, there is no way of proving where "Cosa Nostra" came from. [12]

The origin of Camorra is not clear. Some claim that the term is made up of a word for a gambling game called *la morra*, which is played with the fingers of the hand and by calling out a number. The one who calls out the number that corresponds to the actual fingers displayed wins. The "Ca" part of the word is a shortened form of capo, hence Camorra. In fact, the first documentation of the name comes from a 1735 text referring to a gambling den in Naples. The name actually means "extortion," conjuring up "images of secret sects, mysterious occult powers, bloodthirsty revenge, and an invincible brotherhood." [13] Another possible origin of the term is a Spanish word for dispute, but there is no textual evidence to back this up.[14] As Reynolds observes, there is little doubt about its criminal connotations: "Camorra established itself in and around Naples as a paternal organization, dedicated to providing assurance to the citizens and businesses of Naples that they would not be harassed by anyone except, of course, Camorra members in the event that its payments were not received."[15]

'Ndrangheta probably derives from the Greek word *andragathos*, meaning "a good and courageous man worthy of respect."[16] Sacra Corona Unita has obvious religious meaning, referring to the *corona* ("rosary"). Differences among the gangs are really matters of detail. For instance, Reynolds explains the difference between the Mafia and the 'Ndrangheta in terms of the bloodline requirement as follows:

> Sons of Mafia members may choose to follow their fathers into the organization or not; sons of the *'Ndranghetisti* have no choice. To become a member of the criminal family is their *diritto di sangue* ("right of blood"), assigned at birth. While being groomed for their life's work, a process that begins shortly after puberty, male children are *giovani d'onore*, or "boys of honor." At maturity, they become *picciotti d'onore*, soldiers expected to carry out orders from their superiors without question and without fail.[17]

Interestingly, the criminal organization known as *Mafia dei basilischi*, based in the region of Basilicata and emerging in the 1980s, took its name from the 1963 film *I basilischi*, by Lina Wertmüller. Strangely, the movie had nothing to do with organized crime. It simply took place in Basilicata.

As previously discussed, the term *Yakuza* derives from a losing combination of numbers in a gambling game called *oicho-kabu*, which is essentially a version of Black Jack. The way the losing combination—8–9–3—is pronounced in Japanese produces the word *ya-ku-za*. The term came to mean a misfit or outcast. In fact, the Yakuza like to portray themselves as underdogs or outcasts. Significantly, Yakuza members are called *kyokaku*, meaning "chivalrous persons, men of honor."

The origin of the term *Triad* is particularly interesting. The first appearance of a society with the goals and structure of the Triads appeared in 1644, when the Ming emperor was overthrown by Manchu invaders, founding the Ch'ing dynasty. Legend has it that more than

100 Buddhist monks vowed to restore the Ming dynasty, initiating a guerilla war for many years, a war that they ultimately lost. In 1674, most of the monks were captured and brutally killed, and their monastery was demolished. The few surviving monks vowed revenge on the invaders, forming a secret society devoted to the annihilation of the Manchu. The monks chose the triangle as their symbol of resistance, a shape that had mystical connotations. The three vertices were named "Heaven," "Earth," and "Man." The surviving five monks came to be mythologized as the Five Ancestors. The monks themselves called their society Hung Mun, which literally translates into "Heaven and Earth Society." The society never named itself as a Triangle or Triad. It was in 1821 when Dr. William Milne of Malacca, a missionary, coined the term *Triad*, although, as Reynolds observes, "Resident Chinese usually refer to the organization as *hei she bui*, literally translated as 'black (or secret, sinister, or wicked) society.'"[18]

Triad recruits must undergo a ritual that is evocative of Buddhist ceremonies. They learn secret handshakes and subtle facial expressions and gesture signs. Superstition plays a central role in the ritual. The way chopsticks are held or set down and the number of fingers used to grasp a goblet while drinking signify things of great importance to members. Language, too, is part of the ritual. Reynolds illustrates this as follows: "Certain phrases are used to signify information not to be shared with others. According to the RCMP, who infiltrated the Triads more effectively than any other Western police force, 'bite clouds' meant 'smoke opium,' and 'black dog' was code for 'gun.'"[19]

It is important to distinguish among the terms *Triads* and *Tongs*, which are equated mainly in the Western media. The word *Tong*, which means "meeting hall" in Chinese, surfaced in the nineteenth century. It referred to social organizations helping Chinese immigrants adapt to the United States and Canada as laborers. Exploitation of the immigrants was rampant. Within the immigrant community, groups of people who wanted to help the exploited immigrants, who called themselves *tongs*, became vital sources of assistance givers. After a while, criminal elements within the tongs emerged, becoming involved in illegal activities, from gambling to prostitution and drug trafficking. Wars ensued among tong factions, with the survivors forming a new kind of street gang, separate from the Triads, who trace their origins to ancient legend. The Tongs continue to operate in North America, but their numbers are constantly dwindling in the face of social changes within Asian communities.

Gang names are sometimes based on those of their leaders. One of the most renowned gangs named in this way is the Sabini Brothers gang, formed in 1939 in London. The gang took its name from five brothers who were half Scottish and half Italian. Also in London, a gang named after two brothers, the Richardsons, terrorized the streets in the 1960s. Interestingly, the main rival gang of the Richardsons was a gang named after two brothers as well, the Krays, which became one of the most notorious gangs in Britain. At first, the two gangs collaborated, but they eventually came to distrust one another, leading to gang warfare on the streets of London. The rivalry was immortalized by the 1990 British movie *The Krays*, which revolves around the claim made by the Krays themselves that their activities did not target common people, but that their violence was limited to "their own kind."

Some gangs name themselves after territories or places. The Dover Road Gang, for instance, named itself after a street in London that they have seized as their own territory. The Yardies, who came to Britain from Jamaica, got their name from the fact that they originated in the impoverished back streets of their native Jamaica. The police have been reluctant to use the gang's name in an attempt to deny it the status of veritable gang it seeks. The police see the Yardies as street drug dealers—no more, no less. In Jamaican, the word *yard* can mean "home" or "patch of territory." In the Unites States, Jamaican bands prefer to call themselves *Posse*, a term taken from Hollywood cowboy movies, referring to a group of men armed and summoned by a sheriff to enforce the law. This betrays the intrinsic interest that the gang has for the gunslinger ethos displayed in cowboy movies.

Oftentimes, gangs get their names simply from the world of fantasy. The Hells Angels, as we saw in the previous chapter, probably got their name from a movie or else created it metaphorically to convey hellish fear. The British gang called The Forty Thieves got their name from the book *Tales from the Arabian Nights*. The gang was founded in the 1890s, standing apart from most organized gangs given that it was run by women, who were mainly organized shoplifters based in South London. New members would have to wait for vacancies in the gang to join. The new recruits were trained and required to serve an apprenticeship under the tutelage of the leader, befittingly called the "Queen."

## THE WISE GUY

As mentioned earlier, the criminal's nickname constitutes a brand name. The title of *don*, which is given to a person of prominence in most of southern Italy—priests, noblemen, and the like—is a common one for Mafia *capi*. It is a sign of great respect, a fact that was not missed by Mario Puzo, who gave his main character the title of "Don" Vito Corleone. It is the equivalent of English "Lord" and, in fact, derives from Latin *Dominus*, meaning exactly that. Interestingly, it has become a synonym for "Mafia boss" in English. The first capo to bear that title was Vito Cascio Ferro (1862–1943), known as "Don Vito." He was born in Palermo on the estates of Baron Antonino Inglese, becoming a *gabellotto* ("revenue collector") for the baron and a rich local businessman. By the time Don Vito emigrated to New York in 1901, he had developed a reputation as a capo. In New York, he gave advice to the Black Handers, laying the foundations for the emergence of the American Mafia. He even crossed the path of legendary anti-Mafia cop Joe Petrosino, who had him arrested for murder. Don Vito was never convicted, and he returned to Sicily to escape prosecution from the police. In 1909, Petrosino was murdered during a visit to Palermo as he was seeking collaboration with Italian authorities to combat the Mafia. Don Vito was arrested for the murder, but he was never convicted because of dubious testimony given at his trial. He was arrested sixty-nine other times but never convicted, until Mussolini stepped into the anti-Mafia fray. In 1927, Don Vito was arrested by Mussolini's Sicilian prefect, Cesare Mori, finally convicted, and sentenced to fifty years in prison, where he died in 1943.

Another early capo to bear the title of don was Calogero Vizzini (1877–1954), known as "Don Calò." Born to peasant parents in a small town in the province of Caltanissetta, he initially teamed up with local bandits to ensure safe passage of grain products. He was among the first to make connections, as a capo, to influential and powerful citizens and groups, including the Freemasons, army officers, politicians, and businessmen. During World War II, he collaborated with the Allies and was, curiously, made an honorary colonel of the U.S. Army. He was the most respected and powerful Mafia don after Ferro.

Descriptive nicknames abound in criminal culture. The name of Salvatore in Sicilian is often rendered by the more colloquial and affectionate form "Totò," which is ironically the nickname given to one of the most brutal of all Mafiosi of all time, Salvatore "Totò" Riina, who became part of an internecine Mafia war between clans, adopting, along with Luciano Leggio and Bernardo Provenzano, the vicious methods and activities of their American cousins in the Cosa Nostra. Riina also used the nickname "The Beast," which accurately described his violent character. It was Riina who had ordered the murder of anti-Mafia judge Giovanni Falcone. He was arrested in 1993, six months after Falcone's death. Apparently, he was betrayed by one of his most loyal followers, Balduccio Di Maggio—so much for omertà!

Abbreviated names are also common. Examples include Salvatore "Salvo" Lima (1920–1992), who was actually a politician in the Christian Democratic Party in Palermo and thus a link to the political realm for Mafia clans. He was assassinated when it was determined that he was no longer useful to the Mafia. The irony of the nickname "Salvo," which, although a shortened form of Salvatore, is also an Italian word meaning "safe," was not missed by the newspapers that reported on his death.

Many nicknames are essentially character profiles. An example is the one given to Michele Greco, born in Palermo in 1924 into a family with strong Mafia ties. He came to be known as "Il Papa" ("The Pope") because of the power he wielded as head of a prominent clan known appropriately with the religious epithet of "La Cupola" ("The Cupola"). Incidentally, his brother, Salvatore, was known as "Cicchiteddu" ("Little Bird") Greco, because he was raised on a citrus fruit grove where birds would flock. Appearance, character, and affiliation are the main semantic features used in the creation of many nicknames. Antonino "Manuzza" ("Little Hand") Giuffrè, for instance, the acting head of the Caccamo *mandamento*, got his nickname because of his deformed right hand, mangled on account of a hunting accident.[20] The vicious Totò Riina was also nicknamed "U Curtu" ("Shorty") for the self-explanatory reason that he was a short man. Pino "Scarpuzzedda" ("Little Shoe") Greco was an underboss of the Ciaculli Family and a leading hitman for the clan. His Mafioso father was nicknamed "Scarpa" ("Shoe")—hence his nickname. In a similar vein, American racketeer Joseph Lanza was nicknamed "Socks" because of his tendency to settle disputes with his fists (as in *to sock someone*).

The list of such nicknames is extensive. Among them we find such self-explanatory names as "Diamond" Jim Colosimo, a powerful Chicago Mob boss; Earl "Hymie" Weiss, a boss of the North Side gang in Chicago during the Capone era whose nickname is a slur standing for his Polish ethnicity; Richard "Peg Leg" Lonergan, a leader of an Irish gang calling itself the "White Hand," in obvious ironic reference to the Black Hand; "Machine Gun" Jack McGurn, implicated in the St. Valentine's Day massacre, whose name is an obvious reference to his profession of hitman; Jimmy "The Weasel" Fratianno, a hitman who turned state's evidence, hence the term *weasel*; Sammy "The Bull" Gravano, a hitman for John Gotti who testified against his boss to save himself; and Joseph "Crazy Joe" Gallo, a maniacal killer who was part of a Brooklyn gang with his brothers. There is even a case of someone borrowing from television, namely, Joseph Caridi, an alleged member of the Lucchese crime family who is also known as "the Tony Soprano of Long Island."

One of the most terror-producing names in Mafia history is the one that was given to brutal Black Hander Ignazio Saietta (1877–1944), considered to be one of the most deadly gangsters of all time, who used torture as a primary method of extortion. He was aptly called "Lupo the Wolf," with the word *lupo* itself meaning "wolf" in Italian. Fear of wolves is endemic in Italian culture, and Saietta was perceived as having a wolverine nature. His stare alone, like that of a wolf, was said to have made people faint. He was suspected of having carried out more than sixty murders but was never convicted of any of them, showing again his *lupo* qualities.

Lunde perceptively explains the etiology of Mafia nicknames as follows:

> Mafia underworld nicknames are self-explanatory, usually based on some notable mental or physical characteristic or inspired by their real last name, like "Tony Pro" (Anthony Provenzano). In the case of Murray Llewellyn Humphreys, "The Hump" and "The Camel" are both a play on the first syllable of his last name and the fact that he always wore camel hair overcoats. "Happy" Malone was a dreaded killer who never smiled. Sam "Golf Bag" Hunt carried his favorite weapon, a semiautomatic shotgun, in his golf bag. He was also a very good golfer. The "Gurrah" in Jacob Shapiro is simply Brooklynese dialect for "Get out of here," which Shapiro used to say to resident union officials when taking over their local branch. Tony "Ducks"

Corallo somehow always ducked convictions. "Scarface" was a nickname bestowed on Capone by the media. It would not have been wise to address him as such. His friends called him "Snorky."[21]

A nickname is a marker of self-importance, braggadocio, and fanfaronade. Many criminals try to live up to their names, perhaps fulfilling the omen present in their name. An example is the Sicilian Michele "The Cobra" Cavataio, a brutal killer who got his nickname from his deceitfulness and the fact the he carried a Colt Cobra revolver. He acted and lived his life as a snake might, sneakily, yet viciously, when disturbed. The Palermo bosses had decided to get rid of him in 1969 because he was seen to be a loose cannon. In a gunfight, Cavataio was eventually killed.

## THE TALK

Such Mafia terms as *pentito, Mano Nera, pizzo,* and others are part of a lexicon that is called "criminal argot" or "cant" by linguists. These allow criminals to communicate with one another so that others will not be able to understand. The first dictionary of a criminal cant was published in 1819, compiled by an English nobleman, James Hardy Vaux, who had spent his early life in London and Liverpool and had become a criminal because of his addiction to gambling. Vaux probably recorded the cant spoken by English criminals and wrote the dictionary to gain a pardon, which he received in 1820. Historical documents show that various forms of criminal cants were spoken centuries prior to Vaux's book, many going back to the medieval period. Interestingly, the newspapers reported in June 2009 that inmates in an English prison (Buckley Hall Prison in Rochdale) were using an "Elizabethan cant" as a vehicle of communication amongst themselves, so that guards would not be able to understand them. The criminals were fluent in a thieves' cant that was used by sixteenth-century rogues to keep their operations secret. They had adopted the same type of slang, updating it to refer to drugs and other kinds of criminal activities. The examples reported included *chat* or *onick* for "heroin," *cawbe* for "crack cocaine," and *inick* for "phone or mobile phone."

Whether communicating orally or in writing or spraying painted words on walls or buildings, criminal gangs have always used cant for secrecy, identity, group solidarity, and even historical documentation. A classic example is the cant used by the Russian Mafia. The following list, cited in Lunde, provides a linguistic portrait of the gang's origins, training ground, structure, experiences, and activities:

*akademiya*: (Literally "academy.") Refers to the prison where the thief (*Vory v Zakone*) learns his trade.

*bandity*: A military word for criminals.

*dan*: The Russian equivalent of the *pizzo*, or extortion money.

*krestnii otets*: The boss or godfather of the clan.

*Krysha*: (Literally "root.") Refers to the protection provided after someone has paid the extortion money.

*nayekhat*: Denotes the activity of collecting the extortion money.

*pakhan*: The gang leader.

*panama*: The descriptive English name given to the dummy company set up to launder extortion money.

*skhoda*: A gang meeting.

*suka*: (Literally "bitch.") The Russian equivalent of the *pentito*; the snitch or traitor.

*torpedo*: The descriptive English word used to label a contract killer.

*vorovskoi obschak*: The communal fund that gang members can access in time of need.[22]

Like the Russian Mafia, the Yakuza has developed its own vocabulary that allows members to speak about people and events in meaningful, group-based ways. The following is an illustrative list:

*bosozoku*: Refers to a youthful motorcycle gang, which constitutes a source of recruitment for the Yakuza.

*burakumin*: Denotes a group against which discrimination is aimed and thus constituting another source of recruitment.

*giri*: Designates the traditional Japanese sense of obligation, applied, of course, to Yakuza members.

*oyabun-kobun*: The father-child relation that undergirds the hierarchical structure and overall philosophy of the Yakuza.

*sokaiya*: Refers to common thugs and extortionists.

*yubitsume*: Indicates the requirement of an unfaithful or disloyal
Yakuza member to cut off part of his finger and present it to the
leader as a sign of asking for forgiveness.[23]

Facing unique dilemmas of whom to trust and how to make themselves
trusted without being detected, cants allow criminals to successfully
stay in business. The subtlety and ingenuity of the cant is truly remark-
able. Starting in the late 1800s, Italian criminal gangs communicated via
a truly inventive method, using *pizzini*, little pieces of paper on which
they wrote their messages. The messages were often encrypted in secret ways, with special words that could only be decoded by the intended receivers. Throughout time, the *pizzini* method became increasingly sophisticated, and it continues to be used today, because,
unlike electronic forms of communication, the *pizzini* are hand de-
livered and thus less likely to be intercepted. There are even cases of
Mafiosi using cryptography. Similarly, a British gang operating in the
Markham area of Ontario, before the Mafia, had developed an ingeni-
ous code to construct messages sent through messengers. The cryptic
language was described as a "language so dark and cabalistic that none
but the initiated could comprehend its meaning."[24] To become a member of the gang, one had to learn an oath of high allegiance and a long
list of duties and obligations. "He is required to pledge himself that he
will adhere to their rule, and never to betray their secrets on pain of
certain death. In the event of any one of the gang being arrested, the
other members are found to do all they can for him."[25] The oath of
secrecy was so strong that, to this day, the location of their hideout is
unknown.

## TERMS OF DISTINCTION

Successful criminal organizations have hierarchical structure. The levels
and roles of the members need names to be meaningful. As we have
seen, in the Mafia, the levels are named with such terms as *capofamiglia* ("head of the family"), *consigliere* ("counselor"), *sotto capo* ("underboss"), *capodecina* ("head of ten"), and *uomini d'onore* ("men of hon-
or"), among others. The Sacra Corona Unita has borrowed extensively
from the 'Ndrangheta and the Camorra, using such names as *crimine*
("boss"), with offices held by *trequartini* ("three quarter"), *sgarristi*

("enforcers"), and *camorristi* ("soldiers"). Some of its nomenclature is based on a pseudo-religious terminology, as, for example, *evangelisti* ("evangelists") and *santisti* ("saints"). As the informer Cosimo Capodieci put it, "The organization is sacred. The crown, because it resembles a crown, meaning the rosary used in church in order to carry out the functions of Jesus Christ and the cross. United because it was necessary to be connected to one another, similar to the rings of a chain."[26] In imitation of sacred procedures, a *santista* must swear devotion to the clan on a Bible.

Of all the terms used by Mafiosi, perhaps the most interesting one is that of *picciotto*, the term denoting foot soldiers. It means, literally, "little one," and the suffix *-otto* gives the word an endearing quality. This name fits in perfectly with the concept of the Mafia as a family, with older leaders at the top and younger ones, *picciotti*, at the bottom, thus emphasizing the Mafia's family structure, whereby the younger members are expected to be obedient to, and respectful of, the older, wiser elders.

The Russian Mafia also has hierarchical structure, which is overseen by the *Bratski Krug* ("Circle of Brothers"), an elite band of policymakers who impose their will in an informal manner. The basic officers of a typical Mafiya gang consist of a *pakhan/krestnii otets* ("godfather/boss") and a group of *boyeviky* ("soldiers"). Membership is based on ethnicity, blood ties, or criminal record, supported by tattoos (as mentioned earlier). Similarly, the Yakuza names its ranks (as we have also discussed) with distinctive names, including *oyabun* ("boss," also "father"), *kobun* ("members," also "children"), *saiko komon* ("senior advisor"), *waka gashira* ("number two man"), *shatei gashira* ("number three man"), *kimon* ("advisor"), *kaikei* ("accountant"), *kumicho hisho* ("secretaries"), *shatei* ("senior bosses"), and *wakashu* ("junior leaders").

Criminal organizations also develop a vocabulary that reverberates with specific connotations. Perhaps the best-known example is the word *omertà*, which means both "humility" and "honor," and thus true "manliness." It constitutes a self-contained lexical "code of behavior," as Lunde describes it, that reaches "beyond the traditional wall of silence."[27] It is part fiction, part truth.

In a fundamental way, every nation and society needs a founding myth, whether it is based on real or fictitious facts. The fiction created by the movies and television not only taps into this, but also takes it in other directions. As Dickie observes, even if the criminals themselves can discern unrealistic elements in this form of fiction, they bask in its artificial light just the same:

> Mafiosi are like everyone else in that they like to watch television and go to the cinema to see a stylized version of their own daily dramas represented onscreen. Tommaso Buscetta was a fan of *The Godfather*, although he thought the scene at the end where the other Mafiosi kiss Michael Corleone's hand was unrealistic. The conflicting demands that lie behind the motivation of a fictional character like Al Pacino's Michael Corleone—ambition, responsibility, family—are indeed the same ones that are central to the lives of real Mafiosi.[28]

Words allow us to gain control over reality. As Reynolds writes, omertà, "like the Mafia itself, was born not from the machinations of a criminal mastermind but out of the desperate necessity of middle-class Sicilian families seeking control over their own lives," and thus the legend of the Mafia emerged because its appalling behavior "is actually rooted in good intentions."[29] The original Mafiosi are traced back, as discussed, to *gabellotti*, who were tax collectors and managers selected by the Spanish landowners because they were deemed to be "honorable men," *uomini di onore*, and "trustworthy men," *uomini di fiducia*. These men were often accompanied by so-called *campieri* ("men of the field"), who bore arms and rode horses to maintain order and command respect for the collectors. From this enclave social system, the Mafia traces its roots, since it is from the *gabellotti* and the *campieri* that the first self-appointed *capi* emerge. When the Spanish departed, a vacuum of authority took shape, and, thus, "only one organization existed to fill that role: the Mafia."[30]

Along with omertà, such expressions as *pentito*, *La Mano Nera*, and *pizzo* define the history and character of the Mafia. The *pentito* ("one who has repented") is marked for reprisal by the Mob. American equivalents are "stool pigeon" and "rat." One of the most infamous *pentiti* was, as mentioned several times in this book, Joseph Valachi, who exposed the workings of the American Mafia in public testimony. Valachi broke the code of silence because he feared that bossman Vito Genovese, with whom he shared a jail cell, was planning to have him murdered, claiming that Genovese had given him the kiss of death. Valachi was pegged with the nickname "Joe Cago," which means "I shit," a shortened version of his previous nickname "Joe Cargo," which he received because he would build makeshift scooters for people as a young man.

Another well-known high-ranking Mafioso to become a *pentito*, turning state's evidence in the mid-1980s, was Tommaso Buscetta, a native of Palermo who was a prominent member of the Porta Nova family. Influenced by a meeting with Giovanni Falcone, his testimony in both Italy and the United States led to numerous convictions and, more importantly, disclosed many of the secrets of Cosa Nostra. Buscetta became a *pentito* after Totò Riina murdered two of his sons, his brother, his son-in-law, a brother-in-law, and four nephews. Many *pentiti* followed Buscetta's example, leading to the so-called Maxi-trials in Palermo in 1986. These had a considerable impact and several important consequences. Lunde explains their accomplishments as follows:

> One of the great achievements of the Maxi-trials was to affirm the rule of law in a democracy. The defendants' rights and legal processes were scrupulously respected. The other great achievement was the discovery of the existence and structure of Cosa Nostra and the proof that it was highly organized. The testimony of 1,000 witnesses revealed a worldwide network of arms and drugs trafficking.[31]

But corruption and inertia allowed the Mafia to get away with it, as support was being withdrawn from Falcone's investigation. This annihilated the brave work done by Falcone and his team, leaving him isolated in his crusade. It is relevant to note that only after the arrest of Riina for the murder of Falcone did a strong anti-Mafia movement surface in Italy. It started in Milan in early 1992, when a small-time politician was arrested for bribery. The movement was appropriately called *Operazione Mani Pulite* ("Operation Clean Hands"), referring implicitly to the fact that various politicians had their *mani sporche* ("dirty hands"), meaning they were in on the take. Operation Clean Hands was headed by the magistrate Saverio Borrelli, leading to indictments of prominent politicians and, more importantly, to a reform of the system of proportional representation that had been the source of the corruption in favor of a simple majority system.

The term *Mano Nera*, as previously pointed out, has a macabre and grisly ring to it, becoming a metaphor for organized crime in the United States. It first referred to a gang of street hoods who attempted to inflate their importance by using a symbol of terror and secrecy. The Black Handers preyed on newly arrived immigrants at the turn of the twentieth century. With the advent of Prohibition in the 1920s, Black Hand extortion was replaced by bootlegging, leading to the rise and spread of the modern Cosa Nostra. As Lunde writes, "There is no doubt that the Black Hand, popularly believed to be a sinister, worldwide Italian criminal conspiracy, prepared the public's mind for the idea of the all-embracing power of the Mafia that was to come."[32] A reporter in the United States, Lindsay Denison, wrote that the emergence of the term in the United States was due to some Italian gangster wishing to evoke terror.[33]

The term *pizzo* was introduced into the American Mafia by Don Vito Cascio Ferro, a word deriving from the Sicilian expression *fari vagnari u pizzu* ("to wet one's beak"), or, in English slang, "to wet your whistle," referring to a glass of wine offered in recognition of services rendered. As Nigel Cawthorne and Colin Cawthorne write,

> The principle was simple. Instead of asking for a large amount that risked bankrupting the victim, it was better to ask for smaller amount that the victim could afford, then return later for more money. Don Vito decreed that no one who could afford it was to escape paying the *Onorata Società u pizzu* for its protection.[34]

The *pizzo* represents an estimated 16 percent of Mafia income and is the primary means for guaranteeing an uninterrupted flow of cash for the daily needs of its members. Moreover, the *pizzo* allows a clan to define, delineate, and affirm its control over a specific *mandamento* ("district"). The anti-Mafia populist reform movement *Addiopizzo* ("Goodbye to the Pizzo") is based on the notion that by eliminating the *pizzo*, organized crime will crumble. "If you don't collaborate, the Mafia is finished," is the rallying cry of the movement. But the solution is far from being that simple, because the extent and embeddedness of the *pizzo* phenomenon is enormous, penetrating deeply into the very cultural fabric of Sicilian society. Top boss Bernardo Provenzano cautioned his minions to be careful in their extortion efforts. Keeping people quiet is a crucial strategy, and this means asking for a little money at any one time: "*Pagare poco, ma pagare tutti*" ("Modest payments, but payments from everyone").

It is significant to note that dialect is used strategically by the Italian criminal gangs. In Italy, dialects have always evoked perceptions of identity of various kinds.[35] Dialect forms are often perceived markers of class structure. In Mafia culture, the use of dialect bears significant historical and cultural meaning. Essentially it says, "Only Sicilian or Calabrian is spoken here, the language of our origins and our ancestors." The dialects are indexes of identity and group membership, and Mafiosi feel fiercely proud about their speech, using dialectal characteristics as signs of solidarity and personal pride in their heritage. In ordinary conversations among fellow gangsters, it might even be considered to be snobbish or artificial to use standard Italian, which is felt as giving the discourse an artificial quality, thus diminishing its overall ethnic power. As Gianrenzo P. Clivio, Marcel Danesi, and Sara Maida-Nicol put it,

> The identity structure is mirrored in pronunciation and other linguistic features that carry social-tribal meaning and import. It is a type of "coded know-how" to which group members are highly sensitive. Speakers of dialects use the resources of the code to make inferences about the world and themselves, to give it a particular psychological shape, and to literally imbue it with "sense." Dialect brings people together, allowing them to gain control of the social world which they inhabit and, thus, to evaluate the world around them, *on their own terms*.[36]

Each word used in a dialect is a kind of identity sign. As dialectologist Nicola De Blasi has observed, to a Neapolitan, a word like *scugnizzo* ("a kind of street urchin") describes an emotionally powerful reality that evokes both laughter and shrewd understanding.[37] The term elicits a specific cultural worldview. Words like *picciotto* and *'ndrina* have the same kinds of effects on gangsters. It is part of the wise guy's system of understanding. In the United States, the situation calls more for "code-switching" than it does for the exclusive use of dialect, given that most of the mobsters were born into a bilingual and primarily English-speaking environment. Code-switching, or switching to the important words of the native dialect during conversation conducted primarily in English, is a means of showing identification with the past and a vehicle for establishing, or at least affirming, group identity. The strategic use of dialect comes out in the 2008 movie *Gomorra,* about the Camorra, which was subtitled in Standard Italian for non-Neapolitan audiences to be able follow the story. Without the dialect, however, the movie would have not been as effective. It brings out the connection to identity that it entails among criminal groups like the Camorra.

In the end, made men may speak a different language because they see themselves as different, but they are themselves victims of the language they speak, for it simply limits their thoughts to criminal meanings, and this constitutes a form of thought control. The names and words used to define themselves, along with the symbols and rituals that indoctrinate them into the group, are essentially forms of brainwashing. Users perceive them as meaningful, but, in reality, they are tools of persuasion that keep members in a cult-like trance when they hear the words, much like the stimuli used to train animals and condition them accordingly. They destroy a person's basic convictions and attitudes and replace them with an alternative set of fixed beliefs.

# 6

# MYTH

Myth is the hidden part of every story, the buried part, the region
that is still unexplored because there are as yet no words to enable us
to get there. Myth is nourished by silence as well as by words.

—Italo Calvino (1923–1985)

The German philosopher Ernst Cassirer characterizes human beings
as "symbolic animals."[1] The initial symbols of a culture are connected to
its founding myths, that is, to the stories that people tell about themselves—how they originated, why they exist, and so on. These allow
humans to share group experiences in spiritual and thus meaningful
ways. All cultures have them. So, too, do criminal societies. Without
them, their symbols and rituals would make little sense, since they
would not be able to link themselves to historical events and thus claim
authenticity.

The movies have also joined in by embellishing and fictionalizing
Mafia history. In *The Godfather, Part II*, the origins of the Mafia are
traced back to Sicily, and the organization is portrayed as a timeless and
mythical society. Michael Corleone's wife, Kay, makes reference to the
Mob as a "Sicilian thing that's been going on for 2,000 years," and
whose origin is shrouded in mystery. Similarly, the film *The Yakuza*
opens with a blurb explaining that the Yakuza have been around for
more than 350 years. Criminal organizations that have emerged in modern times, like the Russian Mafiya, and in specific situations (for example, in a prison or on the streets of an urban center), will invent conven-

ient legends for themselves, which can be called simply "street myths." One such myth is presented in *Eastern Promises*, as we have seen. It does not come from a claim to a mythic past, but inheres simply in the need to reject one's previous life through a ceremony of rejection.

## FOUNDATION MYTHS

Foundation myths are stories that are told in early cultures to explain how the world, people, and significant events came into existence. They revolve around divine personages, legendary heroes, or supernatural events. Later societies also have hero myths that attribute exceptional qualities to real historical figures. Robin Hood was a mythic hero who stole from the rich to give to the poor; William Tell was a crossbow hero who resisted tyranny; Davy Crockett was a frontiersman and congressman who died bravely in the battle of the Alamo in 1836. Britain, Switzerland, and the United States have made these heroes, and their stories, part of the foundational fabric of their nationhood.

Criminal societies like to tell stories that trace their origins mythically, imparting a sense of validity and legitimacy to themselves. As George Orwell so aptly puts it, "Myths [that] are believed in tend to become real."[2] But, as we have discussed, this is fiction that, like any good fictional story, is partly based on truth, partly on fantasy and on rationalization. The reality is different. It is guns and death, money and power. More often than not, the results are tragic, not only for the hapless victims, but for the criminals themselves. *The Godfather, Part III* ends with an attempt on Michael Corleone's life, but a bullet misses him and tragically kills his daughter, an innocent bystander. An episode of the series *The Sopranos* unfolds in slow motion, as Tony's biological family is having dinner. This makes us feel that every person who enters the restaurant thus becomes a potential assassin, coming to kill Tony and his family.

Crime in Sicily was primarily a product of its feudal system. The absentee noblemen needed strong men with local power and influence, who also did not have much respect for the law, to manage their estates. Thugs were hired as the noblemen's personal *guardiani* ("guardians"). Law officials were negligent and lenient and court proceedings lax and byzantine. Many judges bought their posts; clerks were paid little or nothing. Having no faith in the authorities, people looked to other means of protection. Banditry established itself early on as a protection business. By the nineteenth century, it started spreading to many areas of Sicilian society. During the rebellion of 1848 against Sicily's Bourbon rulers, the bandits once again opportunistically joined the uprising, allying themselves to the Italian patriot Giuseppe Garibaldi when he arrived to initiate the unification of Italy in 1860. As a consequence, the Mafia gained legitimacy and power, as the first campaigns against it after unification tried to establish the Piedmontese government as the sole authority over the countryside. But, as in the past, the authorities fell prey to corruption. The fighters for unity had seen the organization as an ally, but those they put in power were as corrupt as the ones they replaced. As Paul Lunde notes, it was the "traditional Sicilian suspicion of state institutions that created the conditions in which the Mafia could develop."[3] Nothing has changed since then.

It was from the culture of the *gabellotti* (the mediators between landowners and peasants) that the Mafia most likely arose. During the Battle of Calatafimi in 1860, the *gabellotti* joined forces with Garibaldi's troops to form squadrons. The squadrons were called *squadre della mafia*, after unification, having become vigilante police forces fighting random bandit gangs that surfaced after unification. As such, they eliminated both the bands and became a silent partner in Sicilian politics, as Lunde explains in the following:

> The Sicilian Mafia, now organized, offered to police the island and save the government the embarrassment of sending in troops. The government agreed, and some of the more prominent non-Mafia affiliated bandits were arrested or killed. Once again, the Mafia had positioned itself between two opposing groups and profited from the relationship with both.[4]

To entrench its legitimacy in the new Sicily, the Mafia developed its code of omertà, tapping into the deep-rooted Sicilian belief in a *potere occulto* ("hidden power") that would challenge visible authority. In a society that was becoming more and more middle class, and thus bourgeois in its value system, the claim to chivalry and values stood out conspicuously and effectively. As the world began to change in the process of urbanization, and traditional values started to disintegrate, the Mafia, and other criminal organizations, sprung up like oases in a valueless barren social desert. No matter what their ultimate aim, one could at the very least empathize with them on a moral level. In this case, the means were seen to justify the ends. Myths about Mafia origins show this perfectly.

Two medieval codices, *Breve Cronaca di un anonimo cassinese* (1185) and *Cronaca di Fossa Nova* (1186), talk of an organization of *Vendicosi* ("revenge seekers") who were hanged or punished severely by the King of Sicily for various crimes they were said to have committed. In 1784, Federico Münter, a writer, while visiting Sicily, came to know about a secret confraternity of Saint Paul, founded in the sixteenth century, during the reign of Charles V, that was purported to protect orphans and the oppressed. From this legend, the myth of the *Beati Paoli* emerged, which, according to some versions, were the predecessors of the modern Mafia, thus connecting the Mafia to the fight against oppression. Even a novel, published in 1909 and 1910 as a serial in a daily newspaper of Palermo, picks up on this legend and enshrines it even deeper into popular lore. Written by Luigi Natoli, the novel became a reference point for justifying the mythic origins of the Mafia. In the work, the nobleman protagonist Coriolano della Floresta creates an alternative justice system to which those have been oppressed and who distrust the authorities can resort.[5]

The 'Ndrangheta traces its origin to ancient Greek heroism and virtue, adopting the Greek word *andragathos*, which had this meaning (a man of great courage). The 'Ndrangheta grew out of a nineteenth-century secret society in Calabria that resembled the current criminal society. Whether or not this is sustainable historically, the truth is that, like the Sicilian Mafia, the first evidence of a criminal 'Ndrangheta surfaces during Italian unification. Italian unity was not perceived to be beneficial to southern Italians. Poverty persisted, and heavy taxation became a veritable burden. Calabrians felt an endemic desire to defy the authorities, even if it meant engagement in criminal activities. The 'Ndrangheta legend was that it first came forward to prey on the rich, making them popular with the common citizenry. The exploits of the band were lauded in song and poetry. But the 'Ndrangheta soon made an about-face and turned against the very populace it claimed to protect.

In sum, criminal gangs justify their existence by looking to the past. This is why they speak of chivalrous brotherhoods (Mafias), as Lunde points out, "of tacit state support (political protection), the sale of plundered cargoes to legitimate businessmen (money laundering), and corruption of public officials (bribery)."[6] In the case of the three traditional criminal groups of southern Italy, an unsubstantiated foundation myth is weaved to unite the three. As mentioned in the opening chapter, all three trace their origins to a common source—the Garduña, a group that emerged in the prisons in Spain that evolved into a secret criminal society whose main activity was murder-for-hire. A Calabrian legend, also as previously described, tells of three Garduña brothers who left Spain after having murdered a nobleman for raping their sister. During one of their forays, they were shipwrecked on the island of Favignana, with one making his way to Naples, founding the Camorra; another to Calabria, founding the 'Ndrangheta; and the third to Sicily, founding the Mafia. The story is an allegory, connecting the criminal gangs to pirate culture in the era of the Spanish Empire. There is some documentary evidence connecting the Camorra with Garduña rituals, but it is slight and speculative. History shows that the 'Ndrangheta, like the Mafia, emerged when the interests of the organization coincided with the interests of landowners, politicians, and other authorities to control voting in an effort to maintain the status quo.

The Camorra, too, sprang up in the 1860s in Naples as a strain of the same breed of gangsters as the Mafia and the 'Ndrangheta, surfacing among prisoners who, after being released from jail, took their skills of intimidation and gangsterism they had acquired in prison to the streets. This is a far cry from the myth of the Garduña or *cavalleria rusticana* that the gangsters prefer to spin about themselves. The Camorra developed into an even more vicious organization.

The roots of the Mafia, the 'Ndrangheta, and the Camorra may indeed coincide chronologically with the recounted events, since these gangs saw the opportunity to gain the trust of common people, as protectors of the weak and helpless. They themselves actually spun the first myths, as John Lawrence Reynolds observes, writing the following:

> Like Sherwood Forest outlaws, the Sicilian bandits created their own folk heroes, lauding their bravery and exploits as examples of gallantry. The most celebrated of them, a man named Saponara, was captured and imprisoned in 1578. According to Sicilian lore, Saponara was tortured by his Spanish captors in an effort to learn the names of his cohorts, but Saponara chose to die in agony rather than betray

others. His bravery became a symbol for every Sicilian who believed
their salvation could be achieved only through loyalty.[7]

The reality is vastly different than the myths. The Mafia, Camorra, and
'Ndrangheta are predatory organizations locked in bloody combat with
the state, assassinating its legal persecutors, for instance, the magistrates Giovanni Falcone and Paolo Borsellino. The stories of chivalric
and noble origins are meaningless in the light of the activities of the
contemporary gangs. They may continue to believe them and spin them
for recruitment purposes, but no one in mainstream society really believes them any longer. They have truly become myths in the sense of
half-truths that are used opportunistically as part of a criminal ideologi-
cal system. As the late French anthropologist Claude Lévi-Strauss
writes, myths are unconscious reflexes that we need to rationalize our
existence: "Myths operate in men's minds without their being aware of
the fact."[8]

One of the forms that criminals have used to perpetrate their origin
mythologies is music. The 'Ndrangheta, for example, adopted the so-
called *Canti di Malavita*, Calabrian folk songs that extol the myth of the
good outlaw, to suit their own purposes, suggesting that they were
"good outlaws" intending to help the oppressed and the weak. Similar
utilizations are the Neapolitan *guappe* songs, the Mexican *narcocorri-
dos*, and the Russian *Blatnyak* (which is derived from the criminal slang
word *blatnoy*, meaning "criminals").

Powerful criminal organizations seem to think alike. The Yakuza also
spin a convenient foundation myth of their origin, with the help of
popular writers—a myth that stresses the continuity to noble warriors of
the past. Like the Mafia, they imagine and portray themselves as under-
dog fighters carrying on the traditions of *machi-yakko* ("chivalrous outlaws"), obeying and guided by an ancient Samurai code of loyalty,
honor, courage, and selflessness. But the *machi-yakko* are hardly modern-day Robin Hoods. They take advantage of human weakness to recruit members for their self-serving monetary causes, including social
failures and petty criminals, providing them with the discipline of a
hierarchical gang—a discipline that these misfits clearly desire.

The Yakuza began life 350 years ago as shady merchants at traveling
fairs. They claim to have banded together to protect the poor of the
towns and countryside from bands of marauding noblemen. To differ-

entiate themselves from the latter, they adopted and abided by a code of honor. As we saw previously, this claim to ancient chivalry and the need to maintain ethnic purity among the membership came out in the movie *Kill Bill* during a meeting to place O-Ren, a woman and "Chinese-Japanese half-breed," as head of the families. Objection to this plan was voiced emphatically by one of the elders present, who stated that the Yakuza comes from a lineage of Japanese "fathers of the fathers, of the fathers, of the fathers of the men sitting here." The connection to the past is also symbolized by the use of samurai swords as the weapons of choice in both *Kill Bill* and *Yakuza*. Like the Mafia or 'Ndrangheta, the Yakuza sees and portrays itself as more than a bunch of hoodlums, but rather an honorable, chivalric society that carries on the secret traditions of ancient Japan. The movies seem to be onboard in this confabulation process.

While it is true that townsmen formed gangs to protect ordinary people in the past, becoming legendary folk heroes, there is no evidence that the modern Yakuza are direct descendants of these "chivalrous commoners." Nonetheless, it is crucial for the Yakuza to maintain this romantic and largely imaginary link to these heroes. Because of this, the Yakuza have been able to put themselves into a distinctive category, separate from that of common thugs. Lunde elaborates as follows:

> Much of the Yakuza's behavior is overlooked, because they are perceived as the living link with a nobler world order. While the public is beguiled by tattoos, tales of prowess in the martial arts, and a belief in Robin Hood-type acts, the Yakuza, armed with laptops and cell phones, is asset stripping or manipulating shares in a completely modern idiom. More authentically, the Yakuza developed from the medieval guilds of gamblers (*bakuto*) and street peddlers (*tekiya*). Police still use these two divisions to describe the Yakuza, although the gangs have since branched out into numerous activities. Many of their traditions, customs, and folklore derive from this background.[9]

The samurai myth is a favorite theme or subtext in many movies in Japan, thus helping the Yakuza to curry favor with the general public, much like the *Godfather* films helped bolster the image of the Mafia in America and Italy. Yakuza movies have been popular since the early postwar period. They are typically sentimental, with the gangsters living and dying with values seemingly lost in modern Japan. Like *The God-father* movies, they fill a void in moral space that the postmodern world negates in many ways. Early postwar movies are known as *ninkyo eiga* ("chivalrous movies"). They continue to have great appeal with their formulaic scripts, pitting westernized, corrupt Japanese businessmen and politicians against noble Yakuza warriors. The Yakuza are portrayed as sacrificing themselves, even giving up their romantic lives, out of *giri*, or loyalty to the clan. Even student radicals carried posters of Yakuza actors during their protests in the 1960s. Exceptions to this romantic formula, however, started to occur in the 1970s, when movies portrayed the Yakuza more realistically as misguided gangsters, pretentiously claiming rights to a samurai past when, in reality, they were assassins who devoured themselves in macabre rituals, having long ago discarded any pretense of living according to real chivalry. Recent movies also paint a more realistic, and stark, portrait of the Yakuza as a cult-like organization that attracts young people because of the powerful symbols it uses.

The Triads also recount their origins in terms of historical legends. China has a long history of secret organizations or clans. During the T'ang dynasty (619–907), Buddhism was prohibited and thus forced underground. The White Lotus sect of monks was apparently founded during this time to fight for justice and the right to exist. It reappeared much later in a new guise, becoming involved in extortion and kidnapping, as it overthrew the foreign Mongols who had conquered China, installing a Buddhist Monk, named Hung Wu, as the emperor in 1368.

Modern-day Triads link themselves to the White Lotus movements, claiming to be descendants of the warrior monks. They also espouse another foundation legend that relates to the barbarian threat of the seventeenth century. The emperor at the time offered a reward to anyone who was willing to stand up to the invaders. It was a group of 128 monks from the Shao Lin monastery, all of them martial arts masters, who volunteered their services, driving the enemy away. Shortly afterward, the emperor grew fearful of the power of the monks, having them burned at the stake. Eighteen of the monks escaped, with five ultimately reaching safety. These are known as the "Five Ancestors," as previously mentioned. The monks founded a secret society in the mystical City of Willows, vowing to avenge the death of their fellow monks.

Until the end of the nineteenth century, the Triads essentially continued to be an honorable society based on monastic origins, but all this changed in 1900, when the Boxer Rebellion transformed the society into a criminal organization. The Boxer Rebellion was a bloody uprising in northern China in 1900 in which hundreds were killed. The rebellion was the climax of a movement starting in the late nineteenth century against the rise of Western and Japanese influence in China. It was started by a secret Chinese society called *Yihequan* ("Righteous and Harmonious Fists"), which was originally connected with the Triads. They were nicknamed Boxers by Westerners because they showed expertise in pugilism, gymnastics, and calisthenics. The Boxers set out to destroy everything they considered foreign, slaughtering anyone who supported Western ideas. Foreign diplomats in Beijing sent out calls for help, but the Manchu government declared war against the foreign invaders. Allied with the Boxers, government troops took over the official residences of foreign diplomats. Foreign guards and various Chinese civilians resisted courageously, until a rescue force from eight nations crushed the uprising. It was clear to the Triads that it would be likely impossible to throw out the foreigners. At that point, Reynolds writes, the Triads turned inward:

> If they could not win against foreign abuse, they would win by exploiting their own people, growing in strength and dissociating themselves from any non-Chinese influence or threat, although they retained interest in, and influence on, political issues for some time. Their most significant move was to provide support for Dr. Sun Yatsen's overthrow of the Manchu Ch'ing dynasty, replacing the emperor with a republican system of government. Sun may have actively recruited the Triads to ensure his revolution's success, an obvious move if he had been, as many observers suggest, an enforcer in the Triad Green Gang/Three Harmonies Society (San Ho-Hui) during his youth.[10]

In a form of twisted irony, the more the Triads moved away from their chivalric roots, the more they refined their secret rituals and symbols, expanding them considerably. This may be one of the causes of their continual attrition, increasingly giving way to more violent and more random street gangs. Connection to a chivalric or heroic past in the case of the Triads is likely to be a truism; in the case of the Yakuza, it is part fact and part fiction. They are nevertheless both pseudo-foundation myths. While there is some evidence to support parts of these myths, there is no evidence to support them in the way they are recounted by the gangs themselves. It is obvious that for most traditional criminal organizations, the identification with chivalric folk heroes and warriors is perceived as crucial for uniting the membership and creating a code of honor that separates them from common street gangs.

## AN AMERICAN MYTH: COSA NOSTRA

Among such organizations, Cosa Nostra emerges as an exception. The main reason for this is that the American Mafia has simply transported the rituals of its parent Italian groups and planted them into a new social terrain. Like any ethnic American group, it has also shed ethnic and blood requirements. Simply put, in a melting-pot society, the Mafia has had to adapt. As Reynolds remarks, Cosa Nostra "easily overlooked any prerequisite for Italian heritage among its partners, welcoming Jewish and Irish criminals on an associate basis."[11] Existing in a place where immigrants of different cultures or races formed an integrated society, it became apparent that it was to the Mob's advantage to open its doors to all kinds of members, although the higher ranks were to be populated largely by Sicilians, Calabrians, or Neapolitans. The meaning of the term itself tells all there is to tell about its origins. Lunde elucidates as follows:

> The phrase "La Cosa Nostra" literally means in Italian "our thing," and it was an alternative name for the Mafia first revealed in 1963 by the informer Joe Valachi. It was a term used by the U.S. Mafia about themselves and their activities. Abbreviated to LCN, it is now standard law enforcement usage when referring to the American Mafia. Organized crime groups refer to themselves by a variety of codenames. In Chicago it is "The Outfit," in Buffalo "The Arm," and in New England "The Office."[12]

It was not necessary for Cosa Nostra to construct a mythology about itself; it could get that from its Sicilian predecessor. It became a more realistic, urban-based organization that shed the rural origins it had inherited from the Mafia, although it did not eliminate its arcane symbolism and initiation rites.

The irony in the growth of the American Cosa Nostra lies in Prohibition. As we saw earlier in the book, Prohibition was the political expression of the worldview of largely rural Americans of German, Scottish, and Scandinavian backgrounds who were devout Christians and wary of urban lifestyles, especially those of immigrant groups living in the cities, seeing their lifestyles as based on vice. For these people, the urban centers were dens of iniquity. It was this rural force that ultimately allowed Cosa Nostra to take a stranglehold on the United States. And, of course, Hollywood and popular culture entered the picture early on to bolster the image of the gangsters. "As Cosa Nostra's public profile grew in the minds of the public," notes Reynolds, "an aura of glamour rose around the gangsters, fueled by celebrity associations."[13] The effects of this association have persisted, gaining even more force through movies and television.

## STREET MYTHS

Gangs that emerge in modern-day prisons or on the streets also spin myths about themselves. These, however, do not look to the past, as do traditional gangs, but to the present, ensconced as they are in a prison culture and street mind-set of brutal violence. These gangs are really bands of organized thugs. Common citizens are irrelevant to them; they are only seen as a source of booty and can be dispensed with tersely. The real fight is with other street gangs for territory, power, and sex.

The new gangs engage in all kinds of criminal activities that the traditional Mafias would have found distasteful, including human organ trafficking, underage prostitution, rare animal smuggling, and vehicle theft. The street gangs thrive on the conditions of modern-day urban life and the aspiration toward affluence and the quest for pleasures of all kinds (sexual and others). In a way, the prohibition of vice-based activities is the incentive that drives street gangs. Lunde puts it as follows:

> Markets will always exist where products are illegal or where legal
> excise revenues make them appear unreasonably expensive to the

consumer. In this way legislators and organized criminals exist in a symbiotic relationship. With each new piece of restrictive or prohibitive legislation, with each new attempt to levy higher taxes on products, the opportunities for organized criminals to adapt to new markets are extended.[14]

The best example of how a street gang confabulates its origins is the Hells Angels. As previously pointed out, the gang was founded by World War II veterans in Fontana, a steel town outside of Los Angeles. The veterans felt a sense of alienation from the mainstream society to which they had returned, which had changed for them and which changed in its own view of the veterans. They felt discarded and lonely. On Independence Day in 1947, 4,000 motorcyclists rode into the town of Hollister, California, spurred on by the veterans as part of a rally. The Highway Patrol was called in, and 100 bikers were taken into custody. A similar rally on Labor Day, drawing 6,000 bikers, brought havoc once again. This encouraged a small group among the bikers to organize themselves in the San Bernardino chapter of the motorcycle club in 1948. They quickly developed their own street story, claiming to be unique as a real American gang, complete with their own new "horse," the motorbike. The called themselves "One Per Cent," implying that 99 percent of bikers were decent citizens, while they formed the 1 percent that would instill fear in anyone who messed with them.

In this case, the mythology is an implicit one—that of the outsider, the rebel, the freedom-seeking cowboy. This is, of course, a version of the more general mythology on which the United States, the rebel British colony, was founded. The unspoken claim to legitimacy is transparent. It was in 1957 that a high school toughie named "Sonny" Barger founded his own motorcycle club, which he named the Hell's Angels (with the apostrophe), unaware that other clubs already existed with the same name (without the apostrophe). Barger contacted the clubs and proposed a merger, gradually building it into the modern-day Hells Angels, with its own initiation rites, elected officers, and set of principles. The club also became mythologized by the movies, starting with *The Wild One*, starring Marlon Brando as an imitation Sonny Barger.

Aware of the need to maintain distinctiveness, Barger took concrete steps to ensure that the club would survive being assimilated into the morass of an ever-expanding biker culture, as Lunde discusses:

Under Barger's guidance they took steps to protect themselves from imitators in order to franchise the Angels "brand"; the Angels were legally incorporated in 1966 with an issue of 500 shares and the drawing up of a memorandum and articles of association, all with the wholly laudable aim of the promotion and advancement of motorcycle riding, motorcycle clubs, and highway safety. A patent on the Flying Death's Head emblem was taken out in 1972. Revenue from breach of copyright cases has been used to establish defense funds for Angels charged with offenses from murder to racketeering. The Angels have also been able to secure tax-exempt status with the formation of the Church of the Angel, of which there are numerous pastors.[15]

Although the Angels now claim to have become a legal and law-abiding club, events tell a different story. The thing to note here is that street gangs like the Angels do not trace their origins to ancient legends. They are born on the street and thus create a different kind of street mythology for themselves, based on a lifestyle and appearance code that identifies them as distinct. Biker gangs similar in outlook to the Angels include the Outlaws and the Bandidos, both of which play on a name that means so much in American history. Although it is of Old Norse origin, the word *outlaw* brings to mind cattle rustlers and gunslingers of the Wild West. And that is precisely the mythology that seems to be unconsciously at work in these gangs. The main difference is in having replaced the horse with the motorcycle.

## TECHNOLOGY

As the late Canadian social philosopher and communications guru Marshall McLuhan (1911–1980) often claimed, culture, social evolution, and scientific innovation are so intertwined that we hardly ever realize their interconnection. McLuhan saw changes in communications technology as affecting our ways of thinking, as well as our social institutions. Since electronic signals can cross borders virtually unimpeded, McLuhan characterized the world that was being united by electronic media as the "global village." Current Internet technologies have changed how we process information, interact, and communicate. Everyone has had to adapt. This includes the Mafia, which is now going online more and more to pursue its objectives. But, at the same time, the new technologies have empowered people more than ever before to fight the criminals. One can gain support against criminal gangs by using Facebook and other social media. Because it is not dependent on space and time, such media create problems for criminal organizations that depend on localizing their targets and defending themselves through physical intimidation. Victims of extortion who lack confidence and shy away from speaking their mind might be more inclined to use social media advantageously. It is no coincidence that the *Addiopizzo* movement is gaining its strength primarily through such sites.

But the criminals are adaptive. They have entered cyberspace as well. Technology has literally opened up the global village to everyone. As Lunde insightfully points out,

> Attempts by law enforcement and other agencies to provide a single definition of organized crime have been confounded by the fact that the activities of the criminal underworld are, by their nature, kaleido-scopic, constantly responding to shifts in market conditions and ex-ploiting the myriad money-making opportunities provided by the legitimate overworld.[16]

The global spread of organized criminal organizations is a product of the global economy and global digital communication systems. Criminal cultures are no longer limited to having their headquarters in their countries of origin; they have found new locales in cyberspace and are less and less culture-bound organizations. But this is a two-edged sword for the organizations. Their strength has always been in existing on the native soil, so to speak, where they can claim authenticity and historical lineage. In cyberspace, they risk losing this crucial component of iden-tity. As they become more technologically sophisticated, they also risk disintegrating into anonymous criminal gangs.

The claim to distinctiveness is at risk. It remains to be seen if this will, in fact, be a factor in combating the lure of criminal culture. The life expectancy of the Mafia may be at risk if it loses its mythic basis. The world is being increasingly dominated by recently constituted street and prison gangs, like the Russian Mafiya, who do not feed on mythologies as do the traditional gangs, the Mafia, 'Ndrangheta, Ca-morra, Yakuza, and Triads. Their viciousness is now condemnable, not justifiable, as they deal in all kinds of evil activities, preying on innocent young women in their global prostitution market, pushing drugs world-wide, and extorting money through fraudulent Internet schemes. It is relevant to note that in January 2013, the media reported the murder of Aslan Usoyan, a seventy-five-year-old mobster in Russia known as "Grandpa Hassan" and considered the last *vor v zakone* (the traditional Mafia tied to the Gulag system).

The Sicilian Mafia, the 'Ndrangheta, and the Camorra drew their strength from joining forces with those in power. Their purported origin is evident in the archaic symbolism, rites, and myths they maintain. But history is being rewritten daily on the computer screen, changing how we experience it. Russian Mafias and common motorcycle thugs will continue to gain more and more of a stake in the criminal world because they are not tied to these arcane and anachronistic views. The world is changing, and although the Mafia knows how to adapt, it is resistant to radically changing its traditions and overall outlook. And this may be its Achilles' heel.

This in no way implies that the traditional Mafia has not jumped on the cybercrime bandwagon, as have the street thugs. Cybercrime is one of most rapidly growing forms of criminal activity today. Modern-day Mafiosi use technology to their advantage, employing sophisticated digital devices to conduct communications that cannot be intercepted. In 2012, in the Niagara region of Canada, a criminal group involved in the importing of drugs conducted its communications via PGP, a cellular-based encrypted messaging technology developed for the military. Ironically, people use social media, like Facebook, to praise Mafiosi as they would pop stars. In fact, the image of Al Pacino in the role of Tony Montana (Scarface) is one of the most popular images used as a profile picture on Facebook. Ironically, Pasquale Manfredi, a wanted 'Ndrangheta boss and one of the most wanted of all Italian criminals, was arrested when the police were able to track him down through his Facebook account, being registered under the handle of Scarface.

As Lunde perceptively notes, "While many people work from home, using a computer, it is just as easy and convenient for the criminal to do likewise."[17] But the activities the traditional Mafias engage in tend to be the older ones—fraud, extortion, money laundering, drug trafficking, and, of course, the planning of vendettas. The activities of the new and recently formed gangs include everything else, including such reprehensible crimes as pornography of the vilest kind. But the code of omertà has not completely impeded the Mafia from engaging in some of these new forms of criminality, seemingly going opportunistically against its own moral principles. Lunde writes the following:

> Until the 1940s and 1950s, organized crime, in the main, did not include drug running in its activities because it was considered morally unacceptable. However, from the 1960s, organized crime became very much involved in the trade of illicit narcotics. Similarly, until relatively recently, many of the organized crime bosses refused to get involved in the trade of pornography. This situation is now changing, as they begin to see the massive profits that such operations can realize.[18]

The Mafia has a strong survival instinct, adapting to changing conditions in the world. The move into narcotics is a case in point. It actually occurred long before the Internet Age, on October 12, 1957, at a meeting of bosses from the Sicilian Mafia and the American Cosa Nostra at the Grand Hotel des Palmes in Palermo. It was Lucky Luciano who had organized the meeting. Cosa Nostra was represented by Joe Bonanno and others; the Sicilians were represented by Genco Russo and a few others. The agenda of the meeting was to organize a move into the international narcotics trade, which was a growing market at the time.

Although the Mafia clans on both sides of the Atlantic by and large opposed drug trafficking as a legitimate enterprise, given the code of omertà, they gradually gave in, allowing profit to override honor. Hypocrisy has always been rampant among thieves. The Mafia is no exception. Luciano got around the code by simply suggesting a conglomerate of more than 150 clans who agreed to the new enterprise, calling it La Cupola, headed by "Little Bird" Greco and twelve members. The Cupola thrived, but the new fragmentary structure of the Mafia eventually shattered the peace among the clans and an internecine war broke out over the traditional and modern visions of the code. Violence ensued, leading to the demise of La Cupola. But the structure of the Mafia was changing, moving away from it rural nature to more urbanized versions of itself. In time, the drug traffickers won out. In 1981, under the leadership of Totò Riina, they started assassinating those opposed to the new world order. As Reynolds notes, events such as this "trace the fall of one of the world's most powerful secret societies from a zenith of authority and dominance down to a band of disorganized thugs, many of whose exploits would be humorous if they were not so deadly."[19]

# 7

# CONCLUSION

The main objective of this book has been to provide a profile of the made man and the symbolic entrapments laid out by criminal organizations (initiation rites, names, myths, and so on) to recruit young men. By understanding what the traps are, it becomes easier to see through them and deconstruct the mystique of Mafia culture. The *Addiomafia* can then be guided by a process of unmasking the criminal emperors as having no clothes.

Why is Mafia culture still so attractive to so many young people? Such legendary outlaws as Robin Hood, Jesse James, Billy the Kid, Bonnie and Clyde, Al Capone, and many others are glorified in film, song, and legend. They appeal to an inner need—a "need to emphasize the chaos created by criminals in order to grasp the benefits of order."[1] Outlaws are appealing because we both fear and admire them. Their life is always at risk, but it is an exciting life, not a boring one. Every moment of their existence is pregnant with danger and change.[2] The underworld has a strong magnetism to it. As Jean Genet once put it, by "repudiating the virtues" of our boring everyday world, "criminals agree to organize a forbidden universe."[3]

The gangster lifestyle is a "live wire" lifestyle. Like any live wire act in a circus, it is exciting, thrilling, and felt to be a form of escape from boredom and routine. Origin myths in secret societies add to the mystery of the outlaws, enhancing the excitement even more. John Lawrence Reynolds notes that this lure may lie in affluence, in that affluent societies are more intrigued by them than poorer ones:

Their entertainment value is obvious, but we may also need threats to our security in order to fully appreciate it. In the process, we speculate about things we cannot explain, and often become fixed on threats and events well removed from our day-to-day lives. It's more comforting that way, which perhaps explains why the greatest concentration of secret society concerns rests in urban Europe and affluent North America, whose residents have the most to lose materially and spiritually.[4]

Criminal cultures continue to thrive in affluent areas of the world because they are attractive to largely bored youths who are seeking a form of escape from the ennui through gang membership. But this theory does not explain how criminal societies came into being or why their reach has become truly extensive. Boredom and escapism are factors, of course, but even more powerful factors are the attainment of power, sex, and money. The real achievement for the Mafioso is to see people lower their heads before him and cower at his presence. But power without a code of omertà would quickly dissipate, since it would be seen as part of street hooliganism.

But even this does not explain why criminal organizations like the Mafia persist. As we argue in this book, the likely reason is to be found in the instinct for symbolism that guides human beings unconsciously throughout life and the influence of cinema and television. Portrayals of criminal thugs on the screen has given rise to an unconscious "Godfather culture." And this type of fantasy is more believable than the reality, as Reynolds so eloquently notes, because it filters out unsavory reality:

> Viewers of *The Godfather* left the movie theater feeling that they had acquired an insight into the operations of Cosa Nostra, but few felt any new threat to their lives. Both the film and the book it was based upon ignored the historic heritage behind the organization, choosing to focus on actions of ruthless criminals united by blood and marriage who saw their work as simply a means of doing business. The groups were real, but the threat, while also real, remained distant, and the Mafia's historical roots were never addressed.[5]

While a gang like the Hells Angels is born from antagonism to certain social conditions, it grew into a mythic organization because of the movies and various tabloid media exploiting outlaw culture as entertainment. Outlaw culture offers an outlet for imaginary escape. As John Dickie writes with reference to the opera *Cavalleria rusticana*, the time has come to see through the lure of criminal mythology:

> What is less known about *Cavalleria* is that its story is the purest, most anodyne form of a myth about Sicily and the Mafia, a myth that was something akin to the official ideology of the Sicilian Mafia for nearly a century and a half. The Mafia was not an organization, it was believed, but a sense of defiant pride and honor, rooted deep in the identity of every Sicilian. The notion of "rustic chivalry" stood square against the idea that the Mafia might even have a history worthy of the name. Today, it is impossible to tell the story of the Mafia without reckoning with the power of that same myth.[6]

Bombings, murders, drug trafficking, and the assassination of Giovanni Falcone have contributed somewhat to shattering the myth of rustic chivalry. No one really believes the myth any longer, but it endures because of the reasons given in this book. The idea of omertà is so intrinsic to Mafiosi that it is used as a beacon in a world of dishonor and putrid secularism, as they call it. As a case in point, the day of the memorial service for a Mafia boss, Calogero Vizzini, who died on July 10, 1954, a ceremonial text was hung over the church door of Villalba. On it, the following words could be found:

> With the ability of a genius, he raised the fortunes of the noble family. Clear-eyed, dynamic, untiring, he gave farm laborers and soulful workers prosperity. Constantly worked for the good and made his name highly respected in Italy and beyond. Great in his enterprises, much greater still in misfortune, he always kept smiling, and today in the peace of Christ, reunited with death's majesty, he receives from all of his friends, and even from his enemies, the finest testimonial. He was a *galantuomo* ("true gentleman").[7]

In this citation, one can discern the need for men of honor to be perceived as honorable and thus to be respected. That is the strongest motivation for criminality, and can even be seen in pop culture domains such as in youth slang referring to the "dis" or the "dishonor" as one of the strongest instigations for revenge.

Our view is that the best approach to criminal culture is to ignore it. The moment that it is no longer glorified on the screen, on the printed page, and in other media, it will die its own death by turning criminals back into mere criminals, not chivalric warriors. Even though criminals now form mergers, like legitimate corporations do, they are still criminals, and, unlike a real code of omertà, there really is no honor among thieves, as the proverb so cogently informs us.

Take the case of Giovanni Brusca, known as *Lo Scannacristiani*, which literally means "he who cuts the throats of Christians," with the latter term, *cristiano*, generally meaning "any good person" in Italian. Brusca was a hitman for Totò Riina. Among his many criminal activities, he ordered the murder of Santino Di Matteo's son, because the father had turned state witness. The child, Giuseppe, was kidnapped and held for twenty-six months in a basement. He then had the boy strangled and his corpse dissolved in acid. Brusca lived in luxury. The police officers who arrested him in May 1996 found a wardrobe filled with designer clothes, cell phones, Cartier watches, jewelry, and other pleasures of the affluent lifestyle he so obviously enjoyed. While in jail, he confessed to having murdered more than 100 people. Brusca is what the Mafia, and any criminal gang, is all about—a man "made" into a hardened brute. Dickie elaborates as follows:

> The terrifying thing about the Sicilian Mafia is that men like "Lo Scannacristiani" are not deranged. Nor are their actions incompatible with the code of honor or, indeed, with being a husband or father in Cosa Nostra's view. Until the day he decided to turn state's evidence and tell his story, nothing that Brusca did, including murdering a child not much older than his own, was considered by Mafiosi to be inherently dishonorable.[8]

Not all Mafiosi are like Brusca, of course, and, by and large, the murder of women and children is carried out by Mafiosi only if strictly necessary. But breaking the code seems to be as prevalent as abiding by it, especially when it comes to gaining power. Made men pledge not to become involved in prostitution. They promise not to gamble, womanize, or ostentatiously show off their wealth through gaudy appearances. But they do so frequently, despite the risks that await them.

Telling stories like the one of Brusca, without the myths and many rationalizations that criminals utilize, will go a long way in turning the tide against the Mafia. Removing the veil of silence is a start, but it is not enough. Another approach is to tarnish the image of outlaw culture by demystifying, or, more accurately, "defictionalizing" it, which is what we attempt to do in this book. This occurs in two stages. The first is becoming aware of the mystique itself—ridding ourselves of the mythological elements to discover the underlying meanings. Then we must ignore it so that it can die its own natural death. The heroic and fearless judge Giovanni Falcone observed that the "interpretations of signs, gestures, messages, and silences is one of a man of honor's main activities."[9] Understanding and unmasking these activities will lead, as judge Falcone's statement implies, to an unmasking of the Mafia myth itself. He also realized that diminishing the power of the Mafia was an uphill battle, comparing the made man to a fanatical religious convert: "You never stop being a priest. Or a mafioso."[10] Without a code of honor, the Mafia would have disappeared long ago, as Dickie eloquently asserts:

> The historical question raised by the picture of life inside Cosa Nostra is simply: "Was it always like this?" The equally simple answer is that no one will ever know for sure. *Pentiti* may have talked to the police on many occasions, but when they did, they tended to talk about specific crimes and not about what it felt like to be a Mafioso. But what evidence there is does suggest that something along the lines as this code of honor existed all along. After all, if it had not existed, then the Mafia would not have survived so long; in fact, it might never have emerged at all.[11]

There have been some developments that may herald significant changes. The bosses in American Mafia culture are virtually unknown outside of law enforcement circles, a trend that goes back considerably in time, when Mafia dons maintained low profiles, unlike Capone, Luciano, Gotti, and other flamboyant *capi*. In addition, the number of informants breaking the code of omertà has never been higher. One of the more recent informants was Joseph Massino, the powerful boss of the Bonanno crime family, based in New York, to avoid the death penalty. Still, criminal activities like the *pizzo* and loansharking continue to flourish because human weakness is still human weakness. Luciano left a brilliant legacy for the Mob, allowing the rigid code of honor to be adaptive to changes in society and criminal culture itself. Moreover, the lure of criminal societies will endure, not because of economic conditions, but because of the power of outlaw symbolism and the promise of fame and fortune that it brings with it.

If the lure persists, it is because criminal gangsterism is now an intrinsic part of popular culture, where it is seen as part of an ongoing reality show. The adoption and cooption of Mafia and other criminal gang symbols is now visible throughout the pop culture sphere. A sure sign that Mafia culture is now an intrinsic part of mainstream pop culture is the fact that Mafia Wars 2 is a popular Facebook application and that there are now Mafia museums in places like Las Vegas.

There will always be criminals, serial killers, and all types of heinous human beings, but through the kinds of reflections suggested by this book, they will be recognized for what they really are—street thugs, not knights in shining armor. The testimonies of previous gangsters are also key in stemming the tide. For example, as Antonino Calderone, a former boss of Cosa Nostra who passed away while in hiding under the witness protection program, puts it, "I experienced first-hand the infamy of Cosa Nostra, its violence, its blood, its false rule, its false values, its use of words of honor that are then defiled. My nightmares are still shaped by these ghosts. What I have tried to do in retribution will never be enough" (translation ours). [12]

It is appropriate to end with the words of the anti-Mafia crusader Judge Cesare Terranova, assassinated by the Mafia in the 1980s. His admonition says it all:

> It is necessary to dismantle the myth of the Mafioso as a brave and generous "man of honor," since the Mafioso is characterized by a totally opposite character. . . . The Mafioso shoots to the shoulder, by treachery, when he is secure to have the total control of the victim. . . . He is ready to any compromise, to any renunciation, and to the worst mean actions in order to save himself in a dangerous situation. . . . The consciousness that nobody will denounce him, and that hidden and influential forces will rush to his help, gives the Mafioso arrogance and boldness, at least until the right and severe application of the law will reach him. [13]

# NOTES

## I. ORIGINS AND ORGANIZATION

1. Robert Warshow, "The Gangster as Tragic Hero," *Partisan Review* 15 (1948): 243.

2. The global rise of criminal organizations and their adaptive capacities is documented, for example, in Antonio Nicaso and Lee Lamothe, *Mafia Global: The New World Order of Organized Crime* (Toronto: Macmillan, 1995); Antonio Nicaso and Lee Lamothe, *Bloodlines: The Rise and Fall of the Mafia's Royal Family* (New York: HarperCollins, 2001); Antonio Nicaso, *Rocco Perri: The Story of Canada's Most Notorious Bootlegger* (Hoboken, NJ: Wiley, 2005); and Antonio Nicaso and Lee Lamothe, *Angels, Mobsters, and Narco-Terrorists: The Rising Menace of Global Criminal Empires* (Hoboken, NJ: Wiley, 2005).

3. See also the opinions of Pasquale Natella, *La parola Mafia* (Firenze: Olschki, 2002) and Juan R. I. Cole and Moojan Momen, "Mafia, Mob, and Shiism in Iraq: The Rebellion of Ottoman Karbala, 1824–1843," *Past and Present* 112 (1986): 112–43.

4. John Dickie, *Cosa Nostra: A History of the Sicilian Mafia* (London: Hodder and Stoughton, 2004), 1.

5. Natella, *La parola Mafia.*

6. Cited in Paul Lunde, *Organized Crime: An Inside Guide to the World's Most Successful Industry* (London: Dorling Kindersley, 2004), 55.

7. Diego Gambetta, *The Sicilian Mafia: The Business of Private Protection* (Cambridge, MA: Harvard University Press, 1993), 139. For a complementary analysis of the origins and spread of the Mafia, see Raimondo Catanzaro, *Men of Respect: A Social History of the Sicilian Mafia* (New York: Free Press, 1992).

8. Gambetta, *The Sicilian Mafia*, 140.

9. Dickie, *Cosa Nostra*, 55.

10. Lunde, *Organized Crime*, 55.

11. Antonino Cutrera, *La mafia e i mafiosi* (Reber: Palermo, 1900), 2.

12. Cited in Nigel Cawthorne and Colin Cawthorne, *The Mafia: First-Hand Accounts of Life Inside the Mob* (London: Constable & Robinson, 2009), xiii.

13. See Nicaso and Lemothe, *Bloodlines*.

14. Lunde, *Organized Crime*, 55.

15. Mark Twain, *Following the Equator* (1897; Oxford, UK: Oxford University Press, 1996), 291.

16. H. G. Wells, *A Modern Utopia* (New York: C. Scribner's Sons, 1904), 236.

17. Henry Miller, *The Cosmological Eye* (New York: New Directions, 1939), 12.

18. Lunde, *Organized Crime*, 76.

19. Lunde, *Organized Crime*, 57.

20. For a schematic account of the role of the Mafia in the Sicilian independence movement in the post-Fascist period, see Alan Cassels's review of Monte S. Finkelstein's "Separatism, the Allies, and the Mafia: The Struggle for Sicilian Independence, 1943–1948," *American Historical Review* 104 (1999): 1,789–90.

21. Lunde, *Organized Crime*, 130.

22. A good account of the social influence of the Mafia in Chicago can be found in Humbert S. Nelli, *Italians and Crime in Chicago: The Formative Years, 1890–1920* (Chicago: University of Chicago Press, 1969).

23. An in-depth treatment of the Mafia's role in the foundation of Las Vegas and the consequent "guilt-by-association" syndrome that resulted with regard to all Italian Americans is the one by Alan Balboni, *Beyond the Mafia: Italian Americans and the Development of Las Vegas* (Reno: University of Nevada Press, 2006).

24. Lunde, *Organized Crime*, 44.

25. Al Capone, interview, c. 1930, with Claud Cockburn, published in *Cockburn Sums Up: An Autobiography* (New York: Quartet Books, 1981), 225.

26. Robert T. Anderson, "From Mafia to Cosa Nostra," *American Journal of Sociology* 71 (1965): 302–10.

27. See also Michele Pantaleone, *Il sasso in bocca: Mafia e Cosa Nostra* (Bologna: Cappelli, 1970).

28. Press release from U.S. Attorney's Office, Southern District of New York, September 17, 2008.

29. Jonathan Kwitny, "Vicious Circles: The Mafia in the Marketplace," *Michigan Law Review* 79 (1981): 925, 928.

30. See Federico Varese, *The Russian Mafia: Private Protection in a New Market Economy* (Oxford, UK: Blackwell: 2004). For a more generic analysis of the role of the Russian Mob on American culture, see James O. Finckenauer and Elin J. Waring, *Russian Mafia in American Immigration, Culture, and Crime* (Boston: Northeastern Press, 2000).

31. Lunde, *Organized Crime*, 11.

32. Jack E. Reece, "Fascism, the Mafia, and the Emergence of Sicilian Separatism, 1919–1943," *Journal of Modern History* 45 (1973): 261–76.

33. Dwight C. Smith Jr., "Mafia: The Prototypical Alien Conspiracy," *Annals of the American Academy of Political and Social Science* 423 (1976): 75–88.

34. Humbert S. Nelli, *The Business of Crime: Italians and Syndicate Crime in the United States* (Chicago: University of Chicago Press, 1976).

35. Overall treatments of the extent to which the Mafia has been a corrupting force in the United States are the books by George C. S. Benson, *Political Corruption in America* (Boston: Houghton Mifflin, 1978) and Bill Freeman and Marsha Hewitt, *Their Town: The Mafia, the Media, and the Party Machine* (Toronto: James Lorimer, 1979).

36. Shana Alexander, *The Pizza Connection: Lawyers, Drugs, and the Mafia* (London: W. H. Allen, 1969).

37. Mike La Sorte, "Cosa Nostra Power in Sicily," accessed November 12, 2011, www.americanMafia.com/Feature_Articles_445.html (October 2009).

38. "Feds Allege Mafia Scheme Involving World Trade Center Ground Zero Site," accessed November 5, 2011, www.freerepublic.com/focus/f-blog gers/2467532/posts (May 2010).

39. Lunde, *Organized Crime*, 38.

40. Cited in Lunde, *Organized Crime*, 17.

41. Cited in Lunde, *Organized Crime*, 56.

42. John Lawrence Reynolds, *Shadow People: Inside History's Most Notorious Secret Societies* (Toronto: Key Porter Books, 2006), 181.

43. Tom Behan, *See Naples and Die: The Camorra and Organized Crime* (London: I. B. Tauris, 2002).

44. See Raimondo Catanzaro, "Enforcers, Entrepreneurs, and Survivors: How the Mafia Has Adapted to Change," *British Journal of Sociology* 36 (1985): 34–57.

45. Jean Genet, *The Thief's Journal* (London: Blond, 1965), 29.

46. Michel Foucault, *Discipline and Punish: The Birth of the Prison* (New York: Vintage, 1975), 129.

## 2. HONOR

1. John Dickie, *Cosa Nostra: A History of the Sicilian Mafia* (London: Hodder and Stoughton, 2004), xiii–xvii.

2. Alexis de Tocqueville, *Democracy in America* (1840; New York: Signet Classics, 2001), 160.

3. Dickie, *Cosa Nostra*, xiv.

4. Aldous Huxley, *Beyond the Mexique Bay* (London: Paladin, 1934), 12.

5. Cited in Nicola Gratteri and Antonio Nicaso, *Dire e non dire* (Milano: Mondadori, 2012), 36.

6. Paul Lunde, *Organized Crime: An Inside Guide to the World's Most Successful Industry* (London: Dorling Kindersley, 2004).

7. In Nicola Gratteri and Antonio Nicaso, *La mafia fa schifo* (Milano: Mondadori, 2011), 7.

8. Dickie, *Cosa Nostra*, 13.

9. Letizia Paoli, *Mafia Brotherhoods: Organized Crime, Italian Style* (New York: Oxford University Press, 2003).

10. Jean de La Bruyère, *Characters* (1688; New York: Scribner & Welford, 1885), 13.

11. Good treatments of the relation between symbolism and gangs are the ones by Jack B. Moore, *Skinheads Shaved for Battle: A Cultural History of American Skinheads* (Bowling Green, OH: Bowling Green State University Popular Press, 1993) and Daniel J. Monti, *Wannabe Gangs in Suburbs and Schools* (Cambridge, MA: Blackwell, 1994).

12. Marcel Danesi, *My Son Is an Alien: A Portrait of Contemporary Youth* (Lanham, MD: Rowman & Littlefield, 2004), 57.

13. Works on gang and cult membership—both popular and scientific—have been proliferating. This is strong evidence that such behavior has become a widespread social problem. See, for example, Margot Webb, *Coping with Street Gangs* (New York: Rosen Publishing Group, 1990) and Kay M. Porterfield, *Straight Talk about Cults* (New York: Facts on File, 1997).

14. Nicola Gratteri and Antonio Nicaso, *Fratelli di sangue* (Milano: Mondadori, 2009), 297.

15. Ercole Giap Parini, *Myths, Legends, and Affiliation Practices in the Italian Mafioso Imagery: The Local Dimension of Power of a Global Phenomenon* (Marburg, Germany: European Consortium for Political Research, 2003).

16. Edward C. Banfield, *Le basi morali di una società arretrata* (Bologna: Il Mulino, 1976).

17. John Lawrence Reynolds, *Shadow People: Inside History's Most Notorious Secret Societies* (Toronto: Key Porter Books, 2006), 173.

18. Carl Jung, *The Essential Jung* (Princeton, NJ: Princeton University Press, 1983).

19. Dickie, *Cosa Nostra*, 260.

20. A good discussion of the romance of banditry is the one by Anton Block, "The Peasant and the Brigand: Social Banditry Reconsidered," *Comparative Studies in Society and History* 14 (1972): 494–503.

21. Robert Warshow, "The Gangster as Tragic Hero," *Partisan Review* 15 (1948): 240.

22. Bill James, *Popular Crime: Reflections on the Celebration of Violence* (New York: Scribner, 2011).

23. James, *Popular Crime*, 14.

24. Reynolds, *Shadow People*, 177–78.

25. Michele Pantaleone, *Il sasso in bocca: Mafia e Cosa Nostra* (Bologna: Cappelli, 1970), 11.

26. Shelley Klein, *The Most Evil Secret Societies in History* (London: Michael O'Mara, 2005), 177.

27. Lunde, *Organized Crime*, 38

28. Lunde, *Organized Crime*, 49.

29. Good treatments of the relation between culture and gangs are the ones by Jack B. Moore, *Skinheads Shaved for Battle: A Cultural History of American Skinheads* (Bowling Green, OH: Bowling Green State University Popular Press, 1993) and Daniel J. Monti, *Wannabe Gangs in Suburbs and Schools* (Cambridge, MA: Blackwell, 1994).

30. Works on gang and cult membership—both popular and scientific— have been proliferating since the 1980s. This is strong evidence that such behavior has become a worrisome problem for society at large with respect to adolescence. See, for example, Margot Webb, *Coping with Street Gangs* (New York: Rosen Publishing Group, 1990) and Kay M. Porterfield, *Straight Talk about Cults* (New York: Facts on File, 1997).

31. Jean Baudrillard, *Simulations* (New York: Semiotext(e), 1983).

32. Writings on Mafia women can be found in Mary Jo Bona, *Claiming a Tradition* (Madison: University of Wisconsin Press, 1989).

33. Dickie, *Cosa Nostra*, 15.

34. Nigel Cawthorne and Colin Cawthorne, *The Mafia: First-Hand Accounts of Life Inside the Mob* (London: Constable & Robinson, 2009), 403.

35. Reynolds, *Shadow People*, 193.

36. Renate Siebert, *Secrets of Life and Death: Women and the Mafia* (New York: Verso, 1996).

37. Jane Schneider and Peter Schneider, "Mafia, Antimafia, and the Plural Cultures of Sicily," *Current Anthropology* 46 (2005): 501.

38. Reynolds, *Shadow People*, 192–93.

39. Friedrich Nietzsche, *The Gay Science*, aphorism 283 (1887).

40. Reynolds, *Shadow People*, 193.

41. Reynolds, *Shadow People*, 194.

42. Peter B. E. Hill, *The Japanese Mafia: Yakuza, Law, and the State* (Oxford, UK: Oxford University Press, 2003).

43. Raimondo Catanzaro, *Men of Respect: A Social History of the Sicilian Mafia* (New York: Free Press, 1992); David E. Kaplan, *Fires of the Dragon* (New York: Scribner, 1996).

44. Lunde, *Organized Crime*, 95.

45. David E. Kaplan and Alec Dubro, *Yakuza: Japan's Criminal Underworld* (Berkeley: University of California Press, 2003), 19.

46. Kaplan and Dubro, *Yakuza*.

47. Lunde, *Organized Crime*, 9–10.

## 3. RITUALS AND SYMBOLS

1. Dwight C. Smith Jr., *The Mafia Mystique* (Chicago: University of Chicago Press, 1975).

2. Emile Durkheim, *The Elementary Forms of Religious Life* (New York: Collier, 1912).

3. Attilio Bolzoni, *Parole d'onore* (Milano: BUR, 2008), 22.

4. Salvatore Scarpino, *Storia della Mafia* (Milano: Fenice, 2000).

5. John Dickie, *Cosa Nostra: A History of the Sicilian Mafia* (London: Hodder and Stoughton, 2004), 37.

6. Report of the police chief of Palermo, February 28, 1876, in *Archivio di Stato di Palermo*, GP, Busta 35.

7. G. Giarrizzo, "Mafia," in *Encicolpedia Italiana* (Roma: Treccani, 1993), 278.

8. Cited in John Follain, *The Last Godfathers: Inside the Mafia's Most Infamous Family* (New York: Thomas Dunne Books, 2009), 25.

9. John Lawrence Reynolds, *Shadow People: Inside History's Most Notorious Secret Societies* (Toronto: Key Porter Books, 2006), 179.

10. Nicola Gratteri and Antonio Nicaso, *Fratelli di sangue* (Milano: Mondadori, 2009).

11. Antonio Nicaso, *'Ndrangheta: Le radici dell'odio* (Roma: Aliberti Editore, 2007).

12. Alessandra Dino, *La mafia devota* (Roma: Editori Laterza, 2008).

13. Edgar Quinet, *Ultramontanism, or The Roman Church and Modern Society* (London: Chapman, 1845).

14. Dickie, *Cosa Nostra*, 16

15. Bolzoni, *Parole d'onore*, 23.

16. Joseph Farrell, *Understanding the Mafia* (Manchester, UK: Manchester University Press, 1997), 52.

17. Bolzoni, *Parole d'onore*, 92.

18. Paul Lunde, *Organized Crime: An Inside Guide to the World's Most Successful Industry* (London: Dorling Kindersley, 2004), 68.

19. Gratteri and Nicaso, *Fratelli di sangue*, 34.

20. George Bernard Shaw, *Androcles and the Lion* (London: HardPress, 1916), i.

21. Leon Festinger, *A Theory of Cognitive Dissonance* (Evanston, IL: Row, Peterson, 1957).

22. Cited from Superior Court of New Jersey, Law Division—Criminal, Indictment, Superior Curt Number 91-03-00052.

23. Lunde, *Organized Crime*, 175.

24. Reynolds, *Shadow People*, 166.

25. Lunde, *Organized Crime*, 57.

26. Sir Walter Raleigh, *The Works of Sir Walter Raleigh*, Vol. 1 (London: R. Dodsley, 1751), 34.

27. James Baldwin, "A Dialogue" (1973; with Nikki Giovanni), from a conversation in London, November 4, 1971.

28. Lunde, *Organized Crime*, 55.

29. Thomas M. Pitkin and Francesco Cordasco, *The Black Hand: A Chapter in Ethnic Crime* (Totowa, NJ: Littlefield, Adams & Co., 1977).

30. Cited in Nigel Cawthorne and Colin Cawthorne, *The Mafia: First-Hand Accounts of Life Inside the Mob* (London: Constable & Robinson, 2009), 69.

31. Cawthorne and Cawthorne, *The Mafia*, 69.

32. Cited in Cawthorne and Cawthorne, *The Mafia*, 70.

33. Dickie, *Cosa Nostra*, 208

34. Pitkin and Cordasco, *The Black Hand*.

35. Cawthorne and Cawthorne, *The Mafia*, 60–61.

36. Lunde, *Organized Crime*, 124.

37. Reynolds, *Shadow People*, 192.

38. Ronald R. Thomas, *Detective Fiction and the Rise of Forensic Science* (Cambridge, UK: Cambridge University Press, 1999).

39. Diego Gambetta, *The Sicilian Mafia: The Business of Private Protection* (Cambridge, MA: Harvard University Press, 1993), 129.

## 4. APPEARANCE

1. Jean Cocteau, "A Film Is a Petrified Fountain of Thought," *Esquire*, February 1961, 25.

2. Erving Goffman, *The Presentation of Self in Everyday Life* (Garden City, NY: Doubleday, 1959).

3. Lillian Glass, *He Says, She Says* (New York: G. P. Putnam's Sons, 1992), 46–48.

4. Ray L. Birdwhistell, *Introduction to Kinesics: An Annotation System for Analysis of Body Motion and Gesture* (Louisville, KY: University of Louisville Press, 1952), 157.

5. John Lawrence Reynolds, *Shadow People: Inside History's Most Notorious Secret Societies* (Toronto: Key Porter Books, 2006), 192.

6. Peter Edwards and Antonio Nicaso, *Deadly Silence* (Toronto: Macmillan, 1993), 17.

7. Reynolds, *Shadow People*, 204.

8. *The Illustrated London News*, October 1987, cited in Diego Gambetta, *The Sicilian Mafia: The Business of Private Protection* (Cambridge, MA: Harvard University Press, 1993), 188.

9. Teresa Green, *The Tattoo Encyclopedia* (New York: Fireside, 2003), x–xi. In *Spiritual Tattoo: A Cultural History of Tattooing, Piercing, Scarification, Branding, and Implants* (Berkeley, CA: Frog, 2005), John A. Rush suggests that tattooing may go even farther back in time to 200,000 BCE.

10. Paul Lunde, *Organized Crime: An Inside Guide to the World's Most Successful Industry* (London: Dorling Kindersley, 2004), 90.

11. Antonio Nicaso and Lee Lamothe, *Angels, Mobsters, and Narco-Terrorists: The Rising Menace of Global Criminal Empires* (Hoboken, NJ: Wiley, 2005), 110.

12. Katharine Hamnett, "Katharine's Cutting Edge," *Independent on Sunday*, March 10, 1991, 10.

13. Lunde, *Organized Crime*, 57.

14. Nicaso and Lamothe, *Angels, Mobsters, and Narco-Terrorists*, 36.

15. Lunde, *Organized Crime*, 149.

16. Reynolds, *Shadow People*, 189.

17. Cited in Reynolds, *Shadow People*, 190.

18. Cited in Gambetta, *The Sicilian Mafia*, 190.

19. Carlos E. Cortes, "Italian Americans in Films: From Immigrants to Icons," *Melus* 14 (1987): 107–26.

20. Cortes, "Italian Americans in Films," 107.

21. Cortes, "Italian Americans in Films," 109.

22. Cortes, "Italian Americans in Films," 112.

23. Cited in Diego Gambetta, *Codes of the Underworld: How Criminals Communicate* (Princeton, NJ: Princeton University Press, 2011), 269.

24. Lunde, *Organized Crime*, 171.

25. John Follain, *The Last Godfathers: Inside the Mafia's Most Infamous Family* (New York: Thomas Dunne Books, 2009), 10.

26. Follain, *The Last Godfathers*, 10.

27. Cited in Lunde, *Organized Crime*, 171.

28. Follain, *The Last Godfathers*, 171.

29. John Dickie, *Cosa Nostra: A History of the Sicilian Mafia* (London: Hodder and Stoughton, 2004), 332–33.

30. Reynolds, *Shadow People*, 169.

31. Pino Arlacchi, *Gli uomini del disonore: La mafia siciliana nella vita del grande pentito Antonino Calderone* (Milano: Mondadori, 1992), 23.

32. Simone Weil, *Selected Essays*, ed. Richard Rees (Oxford, UK: Oxford University Press, 1962), 32.

33. Reynolds, *Shadow People*, 168.

34. Lunde, *Organized Crime*, 173.

35. Lunde, *Organized Crime*, 86.

36. Lunde, *Organized Crime*, 86.

37. Lunde, *Organized Crime*, 155.

38. Lunde, *Organized Crime*, 154.

39. Georges Bataille, *The Trial of Gilles de Rais* (Los Angeles, CA: Amok Books, 1965), 56.

40. Marshall McLuhan, *Understanding Media: The Extensions of Man* (London: Routledge and Kegan Paul, 1964), 23.

41. Dickie, *Cosa Nostra*, xvi.

42. Dickie, *Cosa Nostra*, xvii.

43. Dickie, *Cosa Nostra*, xxi.

## 5. NAMES

1. Frank Costello, "Why Do They Think I Am Superman?" *Time*, November 28, 1949, 16.

2. John Follain, *The Last Godfathers: Inside the Mafia's Most Infamous Family* (New York: Thomas Dunne Books, 2009), 22.

3. Antonio Nicaso and Lee Lamothe, *Angels, Mobsters, and Narco-Terrorists: The Rising Menace of Global Criminal Empires* (Hoboken, NJ: Wiley, 2005), 140.

4. Florence King, *Reflections in a Jaundiced Eye* (New York: St. Martin's, 1989), 27.

5. Pasquale Natella, *La parola Mafia* (Firenze: Olschki, 2002).

6. Paul Lunde, *Organized Crime: An Inside Guide to the World's Most Successful Industry* (London: Dorling Kindersley, 2004), 54.

7. Cited in Lunde, *Organized Crime*, 55.

8. Nicaso and Lamothe, *Angels, Mobsters, and Narco-Terrorists*, 34.

9. Nicaso and Lamothe, *Angels, Mobsters, and Narco-Terrorists*, 35.

10. John Dickie, *Cosa Nostra: A History of the Sicilian Mafia* (London: Hodder and Stoughton, 2004), 271.

11. John Lawrence Reynolds, *Shadow People: Inside History's Most Notorious Secret Societies* (Toronto: Key Porter Books, 2006), 182.

12. Dickie, *Cosa Nostra*, 271.

13. Nicaso and Lamothe, *Angels, Mobsters, and Narco-Terrorists*, 63.

14. Reynolds, *Shadow People*, 183.

15. Reynolds, *Shadow People*, 183.

16. Reynolds, *Shadow People*, 181.

17. Reynolds, *Shadow People*, 181.

18. Reynolds, *Shadow People*, 182.

19. Reynolds, *Shadow People*, 166.

20. Dickie, *Cosa Nostra*, 434.

21. Lunde, *Organized Crime*, 168.

22. Cited in Lunde, *Organized Crime*, 86.

23. Cited in Lunde, *Organized Crime*, 96.

24. "Supplement to the British Colonist: The Markham Gang," *British Colonist*, July 9, 1846, 12.

25. "Supplement to the British Colonist," 12.

26. Cited in Nicaso and Lamothe, *Angels, Mobsters, and Narco-Terrorists*, 70.

27. Lunde, *Organized Crime*, 57.

28. Dickie, *Cosa Nostra*, 9.

29. Reynolds, *Shadow People*, 173.

30. Reynolds, *Shadow People*, 178.

31. Lunde, *Organized Crime*, 69.

32. Lunde, *Organized Crime*, 124.

33. Cited in Nigel Cawthorne and Colin Cawthorne, *The Mafia: First-Hand Accounts of Life Inside the Mob* (London: Constable & Robinson, 2009), 69.

34. Cawthorne and Cawthorne, *The Mafia*, 63–64.

35. Gianrenzo P. Clivio, Marcel Danesi, and Sara Maida-Nicol, *Introduction to Italian Dialectology* (Munich, Germany: Lincom Europa, 2011).

36. Clivio, Danesi, and Maida-Nicol, *Introduction to Italian Dialectology*, 123.

37. Nicola De Blasi, "Conferme gergali per scugnizzo," in *De vulgari elo-quentia: Lingua e dialetti nella cultura italiana*, ed. Rachele Longo Lavorato, 103–14 (New York: Legas, 2009).

# 6. MYTH

1. Ernst A. Cassirer, *An Essay on Man* (New Haven, CT: Yale University Press, 1944).

2. George Orwell, *The Collected Essays*, Vol. 3, ed. Sonia Orwell and Ian Angus (London: Secker and Warburg, 1968), 6.

3. Paul Lunde, *Organized Crime: An Inside Guide to the World's Most Successful Industry* (London: Dorling Kindersley, 2004), 55.

4. Lunde, *Organized Crime*, 57.

5. See Umberto Santino, *La cosa e il nome* (Soveria Mannelli: Rubbettino, 2000), 119–28.

6. Lunde, *Organized Crime*, 15.

7. John Lawrence Reynolds, *Shadow People: Inside History's Most Notorious Secret Societies* (Toronto: Key Porter Books, 2006), 177–78.

8. Claude Lévi-Strauss, *The Raw and the Cooked* (London: Cape, 1964), 23.

9. Lunde, *Organized Crime*, 95–96.

10. Reynolds, *Shadow People*, 164.

11. Reynolds, *Shadow People*, 165.

12. Lunde, *Organized Crime*, 118.

13. Reynolds, *Shadow People*, 165.

14. Lunde, *Organized Crime*, 37.

15. Lunde, *Organized Crime*, 174.

16. Lunde, *Organized Crime*, 8.

17. Lunde, *Organized Crime*, 49.

18. Lunde, *Organized Crime*, 51.

19. Reynolds, *Shadow People*, 173.

# 7. CONCLUSION

1. Marcel Danesi, *Geeks, Goths, and Gangstas: Youth Culture and the Evolution of Modern Society* (Toronto: Canadian Scholars' Press, 2010), 243.

2. Danesi, *Geeks, Goths, and Gangstas*, 243.

3. Jean Genet, *The Thief's Journal* (London: Blond, 1965), 13.

4. John Lawrence Reynolds, *Shadow People: Inside History's Most Notorious Secret Societies* (Toronto: Key Porter Books, 2006), 192.

5. Reynolds, *Shadow People*, 204.

6. John Dickie, *Cosa Nostra: A History of the Sicilian Mafia* (London: Hodder and Stoughton, 2004), xiv.

7. Cited in Henner Hess, *Mafia and Mafiosi: Origin, Power, and Myth* (New York: New York University Press, 1998).

8. Dickie, *Cosa Nostra*, 11.

9. Cited in Dickie, *Cosa Nostra*, 6.

10. Cited in Dickie, *Cosa Nostra*, 15.

11. Dickie, *Cosa Nostra*, 18.

12. Cited in Nicola Gratteri and Antonio Nicaso, *La mafia fa schifo* (Milano: Mondadori, 2011), 14.

13. Cited in Antonio Nicaso and Diego Minuti, *'Ndranghete* (Vibo Valentia: Monteleone, 1994), 38.

# BIBLIOGRAPHY

Alexander, Shana. *The Pizza Connection: Lawyers, Drugs, and the Mafia*. London: W. H. Allen, 1969.

Anderson, Robert T. "From Mafia to Cosa Nostra." *American Journal of Sociology* 71 (1965): 302–10.

Arlacchi, Pino. *Gli uomini del disonore: La mafia siciliana nella vita del grande pentito Antonino Calderone*. Milano: Mondadori, 1992.

Balboni, Alan. *Beyond the Mafia: Italian Americans and the Development of Las Vegas*. Reno: University of Nevada Press, 2006.

Banfield, Edward C. *Le basi morali di una società arretrata*. Bologna: Il Mulino, 1976.

Bataille, Georges. *The Trial of Gilles de Rais*. Los Angeles, CA: Amok Books, 1965.

Baudrillard, Jean. *Simulations*. New York: Semiotext(e), 1983.

Behan, Tom. *See Naples and Die: The Camorra and Organized Crime*. London: I. B. Tauris, 2002.

Benson, George C. S. *Political Corruption in America*. Boston: Houghton Mifflin, 1978.

Birdwhistell, Ray L. *Introduction to Kinesics: An Annotation System for Analysis of Body Motion and Gesture*. Louisville, KY: University of Louisville Press, 1952.

Block, Anton. "The Peasant and the Brigand: Social Banditry Reconsidered." *Comparative Studies in Society and History* 14 (1972): 494–503.

Bolzoni, Attilio. *Parole d'onore*. Milano: BUR, 2008.

Bona, Mary Jo. *Claiming a Tradition*. Madison: University of Wisconsin Press, 1989.

Cassirer, Ernst A. *An Essay on Man*. New Haven, CT: Yale University Press, 1944.

Catanzaro, Raimondo. "Enforcers, Entrepreneurs, and Survivors: How the Mafia Has Adapted to Change." *British Journal of Sociology* 36 (1985): 34–57.

———. *Men of Respect: A Social History of the Sicilian Mafia*. New York: Free Press, 1992.

Cawthorne, Nigel, and Colin Cawthorne. *The Mafia: First-Hand Accounts of Life Inside the Mob*. London: Constable & Robinson, 2009.

Clivio, Gianrenzo P., Marcel Danesi, and Sara Maida-Nicol. *Introduction to Italian Dialectology*. Munich, Germany: Lincom Europa, 2011.

Cockburn, Claud. *Cockburn Sums Up: An Autobiography*. New York: Quartet Books, 1981.

Cocteau, Jean. "A Film Is a Petrified Fountain of Thought." *Esquire*, February 1961, 25.

Cole, Juan R. I., and Moojan Momen. "Mafia, Mob, and Shiism in Iraq: The Rebellion of Ottoman Karbala, 1824–1843." *Past and Present* 112 (1986): 112–43.

Cortes, Carlos E. "Italian Americans in Films: From Immigrants to Icons." *Melus* 14 (1987): 107–26.

Costello, Frank. "Why Do They Think I Am Superman?" *Time*, November 28, 1949, 16.

Cutrera, Antonino. *La mafia e i mafiosi*. Reber: Palermo, 1900.

Danesi, Marcel. *Geeks, Goths, and Gangstas: Youth Culture and the Evolution of Modern Society*. Toronto: Canadian Scholars' Press, 2010.

————. *My Son Is an Alien: A Portrait of Contemporary Youth*. Lanham, MD: Rowman & Littlefield, 2004.

De Blasi, Nicola. "Conferme gergali per scugnizzo." In *De vulgari eloquentia: Lingua e dialetti nella cultura italiana*, ed. Rachele Longo Lavorato, 103–14. New York: Legas, 2009.

de La Bruyère, Jean. *Characters*. 1688. New York: Scribner & Welford, 1885.

de Tocqueville, Alexis. *Democracy in America*. 1840. New York: Signet Classics, 2001.

Dickie, John. *Cosa Nostra: A History of the Sicilian Mafia*. London: Hodder and Stoughton, 2004.

Dino, Alessandra. *La mafia devota*. Roma: Editori Laterza, 2008.

Durkheim, Emile. *The Elementary Forms of Religious Life*. New York: Collier, 1912.

Edwards, Peter, and Antonio Nicaso. *Deadly Silence*. Toronto: Macmillan, 1993.

Farrell, Joseph. *Understanding the Mafia*. Manchester, UK: Manchester University Press, 1997.

Festinger, Leon. *A Theory of Cognitive Dissonance*. Evanston, IL: Row, Peterson, 1957.

Finckenauer, James O., and Elin J. Waring. *Russian Mafia in American Immigration, Culture, and Crime*. Boston: Northeastern Press, 2000.

Finkelstein, Monte S. "Separatism, the Allies, and the Mafia: The Struggle for Sicilian Independence, 1943–1948." *American Historical Review* 104 (1999): 1,789–90.

Follain, John. *The Last Godfathers: Inside the Mafia's Most Infamous Family*. New York: Thomas Dunne Books, 2009.

Foucault, Michel. *Discipline and Punish: The Birth of the Prison*. New York: Vintage, 1975.

Freeman, Bill, and Marsha Hewitt. *Their Town: The Mafia, the Media, and the Party Machine*. Toronto: James Lorimer, 1979.

Gambetta, Diego. *Codes of the Underworld: How Criminals Communicate*. Princeton, NJ: Princeton University Press, 2011.

————. *The Sicilian Mafia: The Business of Private Protection*. Cambridge, MA: Harvard University Press, 1993.

Genet, Jean, *The Thief's Journal*. London: Blond, 1965.

Glass, Lillian. *He Says, She Says*. New York: G. P. Putnam's Sons, 1992.

Goffman, Erving. *The Presentation of Self in Everyday Life*. Garden City, NY: Doubleday, 1959.

Gratteri, Nicola, and Antonio Nicaso. *Dire e non dire*. Milano: Mondadori, 2012.

————. *Fratelli di sangue*. Milano: Mondadori, 2009.

————. *La mafia fa schifo*. Milano: Mondadori, 2011.

Green, Teresa. *The Tattoo Encyclopedia*. New York: Fireside, 2003.

Hamnett, Katharine. "Katharine's Cutting Edge." *Independent on Sunday*, March 10, 1991, 10.

Hill, Peter B. E. *The Japanese Mafia: Yakuza, Law, and the State*. Oxford, UK: Oxford University Press, 2003.

Hess, Henner. *Mafia and Mafiosi: Origin, Power, and Myth*. New York: New York University Press, 1998.

Huxley, Aldous. *Beyond the Mexique Bay*. London: Paladin, 1934.

James, Bill. *Popular Crime: Reflections on the Celebration of Violence*. New York: Scribner, 2011.

Jung, Carl. *The Essential Jung*. Princeton, NJ: Princeton University Press, 1983.

Kaplan, David E. *Fires of the Dragon*. New York: Scribner, 1996.

Kaplan, David E., and Alec Dubro. *Yakuza: Japan's Criminal Underworld*. Berkeley: University of California Press, 2003.

King, Florence. *Reflections in a Jaundiced Eye*. New York: St. Martin's, 1989.

Klein, Shelley. *The Most Evil Secret Societies in History*. London: Michael O'Mara, 2005.

Kwitny, Jonathan. "Vicious Circles: The Mafia in the Marketplace." *Michigan Law Review* 79 (1981): 925–28.

Lévi-Strauss, Claude. *The Raw and the Cooked*. London: Cape, 1964.

Lunde, Paul. *Organized Crime: An Inside Guide to the World's Most Successful Industry.* London: Dorling Kindersley, 2004.

McLuhan, Marshall. *Understanding Media: The Extensions of Man.* London: Routledge and Kegan Paul, 1964.

Miller, Henry. *The Cosmological Eye.* New York: New Directions, 1939.

Monti, Daniel J. *Wannabe Gangs in Suburbs and Schools.* Cambridge, MA: Blackwell, 1994.

Moore, Jack B. *Skinheads Shaved for Battle: A Cultural History of American Skinheads.* Bowling Green, OH: Bowling Green State University Popular Press, 1993.

Natella, Pasquale. *La parola Mafia.* Firenze: Olschki, 2002.

Nelli, Humbert S. *The Business of Crime: Italians and Syndicate Crime in the United States.* Chicago: University of Chicago Press, 1976.

———. *Italians and Crime in Chicago: The Formative Years, 1890–1920.* Chicago: University of Chicago Press, 1969.

Nicaso, Antonio. *'Ndrangheta: Le radici dell'odio.* Roma: Aliberti Editore, 2007.

———. *Rocco Perri: The Story of Canada's Most Notorious Bootlegger.* Hoboken, NJ: Wiley, 2005.

Nicaso, Antonio, and Lee Lamothe. *Angels, Mobsters, and Narco-Terrorists: The Rising Menace of Global Criminal Empires.* Hoboken, NJ: Wiley, 2005.

———. *Bloodlines: The Rise and Fall of the Mafia's Royal Family.* New York: HarperCollins, 2001.

———. *Mafia Global: The New World Order of Organized Crime.* Toronto: Macmillan, 1995.

Nicaso, Antonio, and Diego Minuti. *'Ndranghete.* Vibo Valentia: Monteleone, 1994.

Orwell, George. *The Collected Essays*, Vol. 3, ed. Sonia Orwell and Ian Angus. London: Secker and Warburg, 1968.

Pantaleone, Michele. *Il sasso in bocca: Mafia e Cosa Nostra.* Bologna: Cappelli, 1970.

Paoli, Letizia. *Mafia Brotherhoods: Organized Crime, Italian Style.* New York: Oxford University Press, 2003.

Parini, Ercole Giap. *Myths, Legends, and Affiliation Practices in the Italian Mafioso Imagery: The Local Dimension of Power of a Global Phenomenon.* Marburg, Germany: European Consortium for Political Research, 2003.

Pitkin, Thomas M., and Francesco Cordasco. *The Black Hand: A Chapter in Ethnic Crime.* Totowa, NJ: Littlefield, Adams & Co., 1977.

Porterfield, Kay M. *Straight Talk about Cults.* New York: Facts on File, 1997.

Quinet, Edgar. *Ultramontanism, or The Roman Church and Modern Society.* London: Chapman, 1845.

Raleigh, Sir Walter. *The Works of Sir Walter Raleigh*, Vol. 1. London: R. Dodsley, 1751.

Reece, Jack E. "Fascism, the Mafia, and the Emergence of Sicilian Separatism, 1919–1943." *Journal of Modern History* 45 (1973): 261–76.

Reynolds, John Lawrence. *Shadow People: Inside History's Most Notorious Secret Societies.* Toronto: Key Porter Books, 2006.

Rush, John A. *Spiritual Tattoo: A Cultural History of Tattooing, Piercing, Scarification, Branding, and Implants.* Berkeley, CA: Frog, 2005.

Santino, Umberto. *La cosa e il nome.* Soveria Mannelli: Rubbettino, 2000.

Scarpino, Salvatore. *Storia della Mafia.* Milano: Fenice, 2000.

Schneider, Jane, and Peter Schneider. "Mafia, Antimafia, and the Plural Cultures of Sicily." *Current Anthropology* 46 (2005): 501–21.

Shaw, George Bernard. *Androcles and the Lion.* London: HardPress, 1916.

Siebert, Renate. *Secrets of Life and Death: Women and the Mafia.* New York: Verso, 1996.

Smith, Dwight C., Jr. "Mafia: The Prototypical Alien Conspiracy." *Annals of the American Academy of Political and Social Science* 423 (1976): 75–88.

———. *The Mafia Mystique.* Chicago: University of Chicago Press, 1975.

"Supplement to the British Colonist: The Markham Gang." *British Colonist*, July 9, 1846, 12.

Thomas, Ronald R. *Detective Fiction and the Rise of Forensic Science.* Cambridge, UK: Cambridge University Press, 1999.

Twain, Mark. *Following the Equator.* 1897. Oxford, UK: Oxford University Press, 1996.

Varese, Federico. *The Russian Mafia: Private Protection in a New Market Economy*. Oxford, UK: Blackwell: 2004.

Warshow, Robert. "The Gangster as Tragic Hero." *Partisan Review* 15 (1948): 240–44.

Webb, Margot. *Coping with Street Gangs*. New York: Rosen Publishing Group, 1990.

Weil, Simone. *Selected Essays*, ed. Richard Rees. Oxford, UK: Oxford University Press, 1962.

Wells, H. G. *A Modern Utopia*. New York: C. Scribner's Sons, 1904.

# INDEX

# ABOUT THE AUTHORS

**Antonio Nicaso** is an award-winning journalist, a bestselling author, and an internationally recognized expert on organized crime. He is a regular consultant to governments and law-enforcement agencies around the world and a lecturer at several universities. Nicaso has written twenty-six books on the field of Mafia, 'Ndrangheta, and other criminal organizations. He teaches in the postgraduate courses on history of organized crime at Middlebury College (Vermont), and he sits on the International Advisory Council of the Italian Institute of Stategic Studies "Nicolò Machiavelli," based in Rome, Italy.

**Marcel Danesi** is full professor of anthropology at the University of Toronto. He is also cross-appointed to the Faculty of Communication Sciences of the University of Lugano in Switzerland. He has authored many works in the fields of semiotics, youth studies, and popular culture, including *Popular Culure: Introductory Perspectives*; *Of Cigarettes, High Heels and Other Interesting Things: An Introduction to Semiotics*; and *Geeks, Goths, and Gangstas: Youth Culture and the Evolution of Modern Society*. He was made a fellow of the Royal Society of Canada in 1998 for his research. Currently, he is editor of *Semiotica*, the leading journal in the field of semiotics and interdisciplinary studies.